WISDOMKEEPERS:
Meetings with Native American Spiritual Elders

The Author's of *WISDOMKEEPERS* wish to express their gratitude to all who have contributed to this work. While not every Wisdomkeeper who was photographed or interviewed could be in this book, we wish to acknowledge them all. They have had a profound influence on us and Native Americans throughout the country, as exemplified by Mohawk Elder, Tehanentorens, Ray Fadden. In the words of Editor White Deer of Autumn: "He defends the animals, the trees and the birds with words. He loves the land. He reads the symbols written in the beaded belts and tells the people of our origin. He holds history in his hands. Like all Wisdomkeepers, the words of Tehanentorens speak to those who listen."

WISDOMKEEPERS has been printed entirely on recycled paper and is the fourth title in *The EarthSong Collection*, a series of award-winning books celebrating life on earth. Readers may participate, if they wish, in sending donations through The EarthSong Society to national Native American organizations providing integrated programs of grants, technical training and management support to Native people in their self-help efforts to rebuild their communities. These organizations are dedicated to maintaining and promoting the uniqueness of Native people and Nations.

Please check one or more of the following:

_____ I understand that a portion of the proceeds from this book will go to programs promoting the uniqueness of Native Americans.

_____ I would like an embossed certificate from The EarthSong Society, suitable for framing, acknowledging my contribution. I am enclosing along with my completed form a check for $10.00 or more to help with this program. Mail to: The EarthSong Society, 300 N.W.14th, Portland, OR, 97209. (503) 647-5109

_____ I would like information about other EarthSong Collection books.

Name _____

Address _____

City/State/Zip _____

Phone _____

The EarthSong Collection: Books That Celebrate Life on Earth

WISDOMKEEPERS

MEETINGS WITH NATIVE AMERICAN SPIRITUAL ELDERS

PHOTOGRAPHER
Steve Wall

AUTHORS
Harvey Arden
Steve Wall

EDITOR
White Deer of Autumn

DESIGN
Principia Graphica

Beyond Words Publishing, Inc.

To our families whose love supported and nurtured us during the years of our journey.

STEVE WALL

HARVEY ARDEN

THE EARTHSONG COLLECTION

PUBLISHER

Beyond Words Publishing, Inc.

13950 N.W. Pumpkin Ridge Rd.

Hillsboro, Oregon

97123

503·647·5109

PAPER

Esse, by Gilbert Paper

PRINTING

Dynagraphics, Inc.

COLOR SEPARATIONS

Wy'east Color, Inc.

TYPOGRAPHY

Schlegel Typesetting Co.

COLOR SPECIFICATION

Colorcurve Systems Inc.

INK FORMULATION

Ink Systems, Inc.

BINDING

Lincoln and Allen Bindery

THE EARTHSONG COLLECTION

Books that plant trees, save eagles and celebrate life on Earth:

Within a Rainbowed Sea

Moloka'i: An Island in Time

The American Eagle

Wisdomkeepers

Light on the Land

Library of Congress Catalogue Number 90-083550

ISBN: 0-941831-55-8 Hard Cover

ISBN: 0-941831-66-3 Soft Cover

Printed in the United States of America

Distributed by Publishers Group West.

The information contained in this book is intended to be educational and not for diagnosis, prescription, or treatment of health disorders, whatsoever. This information should not replace competent medical care. The authors and Publisher are in no way liable for any use or misuse of the information.

This book is printed on recycled paper.

TABLE OF CONTENTS

Editor's Note

Today, many Native American Elders must use English in order to communicate their wisdom to others. This is not easily done with a second language. One of the greatest difficulties regarding translation of Native languages into English lies with understanding the Native American concept of a First Cause. ✤ *Sakoiatisan*, *Wakan Tanka*, *Taiowa*, and *Kitche Manitou* are, respectively, Iroquois, Lakota, Hopi, and Ojibway tribal names that incorporate an understanding that all things are part of an incomprehensible totality which always was and always will be. Onondaga Chief Oren Lyons expresses this eloquently and simply by stating that all things are equal because all things are part of the whole. ✤ Terms now commonly used such as *God*, *Creator*, and *Great Spirit* are not adequate names for *Sakoiatisan, Wakan Tanka, Taiowa,* and *Kitche Manitou.* That is the failure of the English language, not of the idea. *God* is a term that connotes an anthropomorphic being who dwells outside of humans and nature. *Creator* is a term that also assigns a male gender to the First Cause and does not take into consideration that there were other creators which sprang forth, such as *Sotuknang* of the Hopi creation account. These supernatural beings—who could create worlds and other forms of life—could be male or female. *Taiowa* and *Wakan Tanka* are not male deities. These names represent the sum total of all things. It is what Black Elk described as the spirits of all things living together as one, but even *spirit* has its limitations in English. The English term *Great Spirit* attempts to define what is incomprehensible. ✤ Reading the words of the Wisdomkeepers, we must understand that these terms—*God, Creator,* and *Great Spirit*—have been used to convey the concept that all things are interrelated and an equal part of the whole: that we are like drops of rain which will one day return to the ocean, that we are like candles lit by the fire of the sun, forever part of it. ✤ The Wisdomkeepers all share the idea that the four-legged and winged nations, the creeping and crawling ones, the plant and tree nations, and those who dwell among the stars, are descended from and are a part of this Great Holy Mystery.

WHITE DEER OF AUTUMN

PREAMBLE

Think not forever of yourselves, O Chiefs,
nor of your own generation.
Think of continuing generations of our families,
think of our grandchildren
and of those yet unborn,
whose faces are coming from
beneath the ground.

Words spoken by the Peacemaker,
founder of the Iroquois Confederacy,
circa 1000 A.D.

FOREWORD

Just off the map, beyond the Interstates, out past the power lines and the shopping malls, up that little side road without a sign on it, lies the land of the Wisdomkeepers. Hidden from the mainstream of contemporary life, these living treasures of traditional Native America are revered among their people as the Elders, the Old Ones, the Grandfathers and the Grandmothers—the fragile repositories of ancient ways and sacred knowledge going back millenniums. They don't preserve it. They live it. ✤ We knew little about such things when the man we now call the Gatekeeper approached us in late 1981. We were in western North Carolina, working on an unrelated magazine article, and found ourselves talking to a local landowner in his horse pasture one afternoon. We'd just asked him if he knew any interesting local "characters" for the article, and he mentioned an Indian, a Cherokee medicine man, whom he thought we might find interesting. Even as he was speaking, the Cherokee slid his battered blue pickup to a halt in front of us, emerged from the billowing dust, and with surprising nimbleness for a full-bellied man vaulted the barbed-wire fence to present his outstretched hand in greeting. ✤ At first, in spite of his smiles and outward good humor, there seemed something vaguely menacing about him. His smile had a way of fading suddenly, revealing an underlying expression that was half angry, half sad. Not much was said at that first meeting. We found ourselves avoiding his eyes. Drawing back, we exchanged pleasantries and said goodbye, not expecting to see him again. But, then, wherever we went over the next few days, it seemed he was already there—or would turn up shortly after we had arrived—always friendly, always ready to talk.

His appearances were uncanny. Eventually we got over our inhibitions, our inner uncertainties. This man wasn't looking for small talk. He had something on his mind—and in some unfathomable way, we two unlikely white journalists had something to do with it. What was bothering him finally surfaced. ✤ He was a "middle-level" medicine man, primarily an herbalist. He had studied with two famous modern medicine men—Amonyeeta Wolf Sequoyah of the Cherokee and Josie Billie of the Seminole. Both, alas, had died in recent months. He recalled that Amonyeeta, just before his death, had invited him to become a disciple, so he could pass on everything he knew—but, feeling inadequate, he had declined. When Amonyeeta abruptly died, the Gatekeeper was swept by a wave of remorse. As a kind of penance, he took it upon himself to make a journey—a spirit-journey—to the Grandfathers and Grandmothers of other Indian nations around the country. He would sit at their knees and learn from them whatever they cared to share.

"The Grandfathers are dying out," he said, "and the old way is going with them. Someone has to go out to them, record their words, take their photographs. Otherwise it will all be lost.

I'm no photographer or writer. I believe you two guys have been chosen to do it." ✤ The Cherokee's words, like seeds, took root in us, and the idea was born of a journey into Native America in search of the Grandfathers and Grandmothers—the Wisdomkeepers. At first we thought the Cherokee himself would lead us into that mystic labyrinth, but we were wrong. Yes, he would be going on such a spirit-journey, he told us, but he would be going alone, going down his own path. For us, he was only the Gatekeeper, not the Guide. He had shown the Way. It was up to us to follow it. ✤ So began an odyssey that continues to this day. Traveling across the land for nearly ten years now, we have sought out the spiritual Elders of more than a score of Native American nations: Lakota, Iroquois, Seminole, Ojibway, Hopi, Ute, Pawnee, Shinnecock, Hoh, Lumbee, and others. We have met them on their sacred soil, entered their homes and lives, and discovered the infinite riches of their friendship. Not being "Indian experts" may have been our greatest strength. Had we been anthropologists or sociologists or, heaven help us, "ethnohistorians," we would likely have been thrown out on our ears more than a few times. We asked for no "secrets," only for whatever they cared to share with us. Quite beyond our expectations, they revealed their inmost thoughts and feelings, their dreams and visions, their healing remedies and apocalyptic prophecies, and, above all, their humanity—which shines through every page of *Wisdomkeepers*. ✜ What began as a journalistic project became a mission. Each Wisdomkeeper bestowed on us some special gift of understanding, some indelible experience. From each we came back enriched. Wisdomkeepers, we learned, are not necessarily "old." Several of the acknowledged spiritual or political leaders of their people are still in their forties and fifties. Others even younger are coming after them. We learned that our Cherokee Gatekeeper had been wrong in one thing: The Grandfathers and Grandmothers may be dying—as inevitably they must—but they are emphatically *not* dying out. As we learned from Eddie Benton-Banai, fourth-level Midewiwin priest of the Ojibway, "The Grandfathers and the Grandmothers are in the children—whose faces are coming from beneath the ground!" ✜ We are changed. We have been seized and shaken. We went out two journalists after a good story. We came back two "runners" from another world, carrying an urgent message from the Wisdomkeepers. ✜ This book is that message.

STEVE WALL

HARVEY ARDEN

CHARLIE KNIGHT ✛ Ute

Out on the high desert plateau of southwestern Colorado, Ute medicine man Charlie Knight sits at the open door of his shiny blue Chevy pickup, eyeing the two approaching strangers whose dusty rent-a-car has just pulled up to his little one-man aluminum trailer. Tucked away behind a low rust-red mesa, the trailer—a cubbyhole on wheels—sits in an almost inconceivably vast amphitheater of stony desert with bizarre shafts of frozen rock rising up here and there against the tilting horizons. ✛ To the west the massif of horizontal Sleeping Ute Mountain lies prone at the foot of the color-streaked late-afternoon sky. Once, legend goes, all Utes were giants. A hunting party of these Ute giants left a lone brave behind to stand sentry over the land until they returned. Centuries passed and the giant sentry at last fell asleep. At this, the Creator became angry and reduced all Utes to normal human size—except the sleeping sentry, who was transformed into a mountain to stand eternal guard over the land. It's said that one day the giant Sleeping Ute will rise up from the earth and come to the rescue of his people in a time of great danger. ✛ Not many white men turn up out here at Charlie's sheep camp. The two-lane blacktop goes by about a mile away, and it's easy to miss the weed-grown dirt rut of a road that turns off at a sagging barbed wire fence a dozen miles south of Cortez, the nearest town. The little Ute community of Towaoc lies a few miles off. Three dogs howl our arrival and slink behind the pickup,

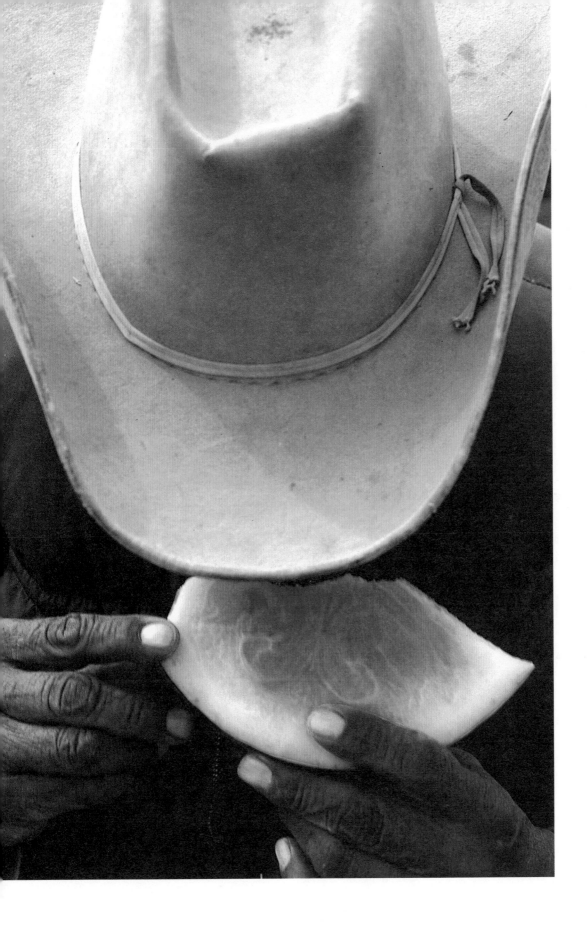

hackles raised, awaiting a cue from Charlie on how to react to these two unlikely intruders. ✤ "When you leavin'?" are his first words. He smiles ever so slightly, eyes unfathomable behind dark-tinted, metal-rimmed sunglasses. ✤ We explain why we've come: We'd like to share with him a few hours, days, even weeks; to record his words, take some photographs, and bring back to the outside world any message or messages he might like to transmit. Charlie snorts and shakes his head. "When did you fellas say you're leavin'?" ✤ We take no insult. There's no venom in his words. We even sense a certain rough and easy friendliness in the low guttural tones of his voice. He speaks slowly, wrestling with his seldom-used English. "How you know where to find Charlie?" ✤ A Cheyenne-Sioux named Bob White in northern California had given us his name as a high-level medicine man, and his daughter Judy in Towaoc had given us directions out to the sheep camp. ✤ Charlie winces at the words medicine man. "He tell you I'm a medicine man? How's he know? Charlie's no medicine man. Charlie does a little medicine, that's all. Maybe you got the wrong Charlie. Yup, that's who you got—the wrong Charlie!" He wheezes out a short loud laugh, enjoying his joke. ✤ "Better go now, you two. Charlie's got to get up early tomorrow. Got to catch me a wild bull up on the mountain. That's me, wild bull Charlie—not medicine man Charlie! You fellas got the wrong Charlie!" ✤ Now, abruptly, he's dead serious again. He studies us through the sunglasses. "Maybe you come again," he says, "but now you better go. Not good two fellas like you be wandering around here after dark. Things can happen at night. Stick people could be out," he grins. "You got the wrong Charlie!" he yells out as we drive off.

We hang around for the next few days, chasing wild bulls with Charlie and his son Big Jim on the lower slopes of Sleeping Ute Mountain, then attending a livestock auction with the two of them in Cortez. They get used to these two prying white intruders. After the auction, Charlie invites us to come out to his daughter Judy's house the next day. "Maybe we talk a little," he says. ✤ Next day, before Charlie arrives, we talk to Judy. "According to BIA rolls,"

she tells us, "my Dad was born January 1, 1909. But that's just a date they assigned to lots of older people during a census years ago. My Dad says some of the others with the same birthdate were still babies when he was a boy. He's probably 85—maybe a few years older." She tells us that a few months before, a revered elder she calls simply "Grandfather" had died. "He was more than a medicine man," she says. "Grandfather could do things no one else could do. He could make tears come out of a piece of wood during the Sun Dance. After he died, they say his power went into my Dad. He can do wonderful things, too." ✚ Charlie arrives, gives us a perfunctory nod, and sits in an armchair, hands on his knees, looking away from us. There's a long silence. Slowly he pivots around and peers at us through his sunglasses. He says something to Judy in Ute, and moments later she brings out a small cassette player, which Charlie takes and sets on his lap.

CHARLIE'S SONG

"Charlie's going to play his song for you," he says. From his shirt pocket he brings out a worn-looking cassette and inserts it into the player. He keeps looking at us as if still uncertain whether to proceed. His small hands hover above the cassette player like two nervous birds. Finally he nods to himself, grunts, and presses the "play" button. Through the scratchy hiss of the tape comes the half-muffled sound of a high-pitched drum over whose regular beat a man's voice chants out: *"Hey-uh... Hey-uh... Hey-uh-uh-uh-uh!"* "That's me singing," Charlie says. "That's me playing the water drum, too." His fingers rap on the plastic cover of the cassette player. A vague sound comes from his throat, as if he's inwardly singing. He has taken off his sunglasses and watches us intently as we listen. *"Hey-uh,"* goes the tape, *"Hey-uh... Hey-uh-uh-uh-uh!"* ✣ After a few minutes he turns the tape off. "Now you know Charlie," he says.

"If you know my song, you know Charlie. Everyone has a song. God gives us each a song. That's how we know who we are. Our song tells us who we are.

And there are other songs, different songs for different things, some for dancing, some for singing, some for healing. Every sickness takes a different song. You tune the water drum different for each song. Little person inside you tells you what song to sing. Little person comes from God, teaches Charlie the songs he knows. You got to hear the little person to learn the songs." ✣ His fingers keep tapping the cover of the cassette player as he talks. "When Charlie was a boy he went up Sleeping Ute Mountain to pray and ask God for a song. Charlie climbed a long time and got tired, went to sleep. Then God comes into Charlie's dream. He sings Charlie's song. When Charlie wakes up, he remembers the song. Little person helps him remember. Little person stays inside Charlie. Always there. Even now." He taps his chest with his index finger. "In here." ✤ Charlie gets up and goes to the fireplace. Lighting a match, he drops it in a frying pan Judy had set moments before on the glowing, near-spent logs. Instantly a sharp, sweet odor penetrates the air. "Cedar," Judy says. "It clears the house of unwanted spirits." ✤ Standing before the fire, Charlie prays aloud in Ute for several minutes. Then, turning to us, he says: "Smoke keeps the stick people away. I think they're looking for you two. Last night we seen them, right out there, behind the house, like big dogs, walking on their back legs. Like this." He raises his arms and struts about like some strange, stiff-legged creature, circling us as if stalking prey. Then he laughs and sits back down, yawning. ✤ "When you leavin'?" he asks abruptly in the same flat tone he'd used at our first meeting. "Charlie's tired now. Tomorrow, if you like, come on out to the sheep camp. Maybe Charlie'll tell you some more." ✤ We rise to go. He peers at us intently over his sunglasses. "Watch out for stick people," he warns. "They gone for now, but they'll be back." His chuckle follows us enigmatically out the door. It's almost night. In the distance Sleeping Ute Mountain is dissolving in purple shadow. Not a little uneasy, we drive back to our motel in Cortez, absorbed in dark imaginings of the "stick people."

The next morning we join Charlie in the cramped confines of his little trailer. "In the old days we had a tent, not a trailer," he says. "Charlie was born in a tent. Judy and Big Jim, too. We still use a tent up on the mountain." Seated on the bunk, he wrestles off his cowboy boots and slips on a dainty pair of beaded moccasins. "For dancing," he says. ✤ The interior of the tiny trailer has a stove, a sink, a small refrigerator, and not much else. Half a dozen cowboy hats are

stacked on a shelf above the bunk. Charlie takes one down and puts it on. "This is for dress," he says, "Makes Charlie pretty. Maybe you think Charlie's ugly. Got no teeth, no hair, no chin. But girls don't care. They see the pretty hat and think Charlie's pretty too!" He laughs. "Now Charlie'll tell you a story."

A VISION

"When Charlie was thirty-two or thirty-three, he got his healing song. Charlie lay down on his back on the ground, hands out. In the vision, the Creator came down, like a big light. There's light coming out and He's got angels all around him, all made of light. The Creator came down and touched me here on my hands, then He taught Charlie his healing song, He taught me how to heal. He showed me how to use the eagle feather to find the sick place in a person. He told me: 'Sing the healing song, then build a fire. Take a burning coal in your hands. It won't burn if you pray right. Then take the heat out of the coal, into your hands, and then rub the person's body in the sick place. Put your hands in water and do it again. Do it seven times. The sickness will go away if the Creator wants.' "

"Everyone got to find the right path. You can't see it so it's hard to find. No one can show you. Each person's got to find the path by himself.

If you find it, maybe it takes you to the Creator. But if you go down the wrong path, maybe you find the stick people! They're waiting for you out there. I'm telling you guys. You better get out for now. I got a warning. Someone could get hurt if you stay. When you leavin'?" ✤ His tone is unmistakable. He wants us to go. We thank him and get up to leave. "Wait a minute," he says. "Charlie make a little good medicine for you. Stand right here." From somewhere he's produced an eagle feather. As we stand in the door of the trailer, he holds the feather by its quill-tip and slowly waves it over us, fluffing and combing the air with it, starting down behind our legs and working up to our heads, then back down to our feet. "Good blessing," he says. "Help you find the right path. Maybe you come back another time. Charlie tell you some more. Right now's the wrong time. Later on the stick people go away and you come back. It'll be safe then. You remember. Follow the right path and take it back here. Charlie be waitin'."

FRANK FOOLS CROW ✤ Lakota

AN INCIDENT AT WOUNDED KNEE

It's February 27, 1983, and we're among several hundred celebrants attending the Tenth Anniversary of the "Occupation"—the
1973 takeover of Tribal Council buildings at the little reservation
community of Wounded Knee by Traditionalist activists of the
American Indian Movement. The ensuing 73-day siege by U.S.
marshals and the FBI left two Indians and an FBI man dead and
many of AIM's organizers in prison or on the run. That it took
place, by design, here at Wounded Knee—where U.S. troops using
rapid-fire Hotchkiss cannon massacred some 250 Lakota men,
women, and children in 1890—has made this site doubly tragic,
doubly holy. Now, ten years after the siege, the celebrants have
marched here from the Four Directions, converging at this forlorn
cemetery on the hill's crest, gathering shoulder-to-shoulder in a
memorial service for those killed in 1890 and 1973. ✤ *E-e-e-e-e-
e-ip! E-e-e-e-e-e-ip! E-e-e-e-e-e-ip! E-e-e-e-e-e-ip!* Four times the
eagle-bone whistle blows from the haunted hill of Wounded Knee—
four times in each of the sacred Four Directions. The frail, eerie
squeal of the whistle lifts into the high, empty, chill-blue South

Dakota sky. As the shrill cry of the whistle penetrates the silence, the hushed crowd huddles together, heads bowed in prayer. A restless wind whips around the pungent smoke from burning white sage presented moments before to the Creator. Again and again the whistle's screeching pierces the air, each blast catching the wind and floating over the vast and barren plain, which is surrounded by a far ring of low mountains. ✤ With the crowd's watchful eyes focused upon him, 93-year-old Lakota ceremonial chief and spiritual Elder Frank Fools Crow lifts high his smoking medicine pipe, symbolic of the original Pipe brought by White Buffalo Calf Woman. He points its blue-feathered mouthpiece first to the Four Directions, then down to Grandmother Earth, then up to Grandfather Sky. His prayer, in the Lakota language, mingles on the air with the wafting incense of the sage and the lingering after-echo of the eagle-bone whistle. In plaintive tones he implores the Creator for a sign—The Sign—that He still hears them, that He still remembers and loves His Indian children. A hollow wind wails hoarsely above our heads like a distant chorus of muffled voices, as if the still-undeparted spirits in Wounded Knee cemetery are adding their ghostly supplications to the communal prayer. ✤ After Fools Crow's moving words, chanting singers and drummers raise a musical prayer into

the wind. Soon the crowd begins to murmur. Heads tilt back and
fingers point skyward. The chanting and singing stop abruptly.
People nudge each other in awe. "Look! Look up in the sky!" someone cries. Our eyes raise skyward with the others, and there, perhaps a thousand feet above our heads, circling, circling on
outstretched wings, the only thing visible in all that colossal blue
dome of sky—an eagle! "Now you see the power of Wounded
Knee!" a voice shouts out. ✤ For fully ten minutes the great bird,
witness of the Creator, hovers over the sacred hill of Wounded
Knee. Then, before tears can be wiped from wondering eyes, it suddenly flies off and almost instantly disappears, gone whence it came.
And the Elder thanks the Creator for recognizing the people once
again by sending—as He has so often done before—The Sign of His
power and love.

AUDREY SHENANDOAH ✛
Onondaga

At the Global Forum on Environment and Development for Survival, held in Moscow in January 1990, Onondaga Clan Mother Audrey Shenandoah delivered a keynote address—excerpted here—between addresses by Soviet President Gorbachev and United Nations Secretary General Perez de Cuellar.

I would first give thanks for another day of life here on this earth. It is another day extended that we may enjoy the compassionate goodness of our Creator. Among my people we could not come together in this way—a conference—without first offering words of acknowledgment, respect, and thanksgiving for our fellow human beings. Now our words we direct to our Mother Earth, who supports all life. We look to the shortest grasses, close to the bosom of our Mother Earth, as we put our minds together as one mind. We include all the plant life, the woodlands, all the waters of Earth, the fishes, the animal life, the bird life, and the Four Winds. As one mind our acknowledgment, respect, and thanksgiving move upward to the Sky World: the Grandmother Moon, who has a direct relationship to the females of the species of all living things; the sun and the stars; and our Spiritual Beings of the Sky World. They still carry on the original Instructions in this great Cycle of Life.

With one mind we address our acknowledgment, respect, and gratefulness to all the sacred Cycle of Life. We, as humans, must remember to be humble and acknowledge the gifts we use so freely in our daily lives.

I convey to you best good greetings from my people, the Haudenosaunee. They made for me a "bundle" of greetings before I

departed my homeland, as is always done for one traveling on a mission to another land. They said, "To the chiefs, the leadership of many lands, the chiefs of the Haudenosaunee send you warm greetings and great respect. May you have peace of mind. To all spiritual leaders and persons of office these same warm greetings from your counterparts among the Haudenosaunee. May there be peace when we meet. To the women in this assemblage—the Mothers of Nations—a warm greeting of acknowledgment and respect, for yours is a very special and sacred mission on this earth. And to the children of many lands gathered here we extend good greetings from the children of our homeland." ✤ Thus I extend the "bundle" of greetings and recognition and respect to all assembled here. This is the custom and tradition of my people. These greetings affirm the linkage of we humans to one another and our relationship to the environment and the Universe. ✚ We have much to learn from the incredible knowledge of our ancestors which was gained long before reading and writing came about. From time immemorial every bit of their intelligence and senses were used. Humans knew and felt relationship to all that lived and moved. Somehow that relationship must be regained. We are faced with crucial times. Changes need to be made beginning now, for our life-support system is being severely abused and mismanaged. ✚ Many people of peace have been persecuted through the centuries. I believe that the time of persecution has passed. The energies of the people are now being directed in search of ways to save Mother Earth. ✚ The founder of Haudenosaunee government, whom we call the Peacemaker, intended that there be social justice in the world. No man was to be more privileged than any other man. All were to be accorded respect. A healthy human mind respects the gifts of life— all nature gives life. ✚ There is no word for "nature" in my language. Nature, in English, seems to refer to that which is separate from human beings. It is a distinction we don't recognize. The closest words to the idea of "nature" translate to refer to things which support life. ✚ It is foolish arrogance for humans to think themselves superior to all the life-support system. How can one be superior to that upon which one depends for life? Humans have invented marvelous technologies. The result has been that parts of the world live in unnecessary and debilitating surplus while people in other parts of the world are dying for lack of food, water, and shelter. Priorities need to be directed so that people who have plenty need not feel shame while others hunger and die. There should be no homeless or hungry people anywhere in the world. Those in power need to address this deplorable situation. We are all fellow travelers on this earth.... ✚ We live in an era when far too much money is expended on the military. Even as we enter a time of increasing potential for peace among the major powers, military expenditures remain grotesquely high. The purpose of these high military budgets must be the anticipation of violence. As a mother I demand that our sons not be raised to die in war. War is irrational, its causes suspect. If we are to live on this planet we must eliminate warfare, which is harmful to all living things. ✚ I would urge the whole concept of nature be rethought. Nature, the land, must not mean money; it must designate life. Nature is the storehouse of potential life of future generations and is sacred. Human societies already possess the technologies necessary to provide food, clothing, and shelter for everyone. The organization of distribution of wealth needs to be repaired, for that imbalance destroys both contemporary and future human life and nature. Western society needs to prioritize life-supporting systems and to question its commitment to materialism. Spirituality should be our foundation....

MATHEW KING ✣ Lakota

A sense of apprehension rides with us like a black cloud as we enter the Pine Ridge Reservation. Perhaps it's the landscape, endlessly bleak—a sullen geology fitting the dark events that have transpired here in South Dakota between the sacred Black Hills and the Badlands. As we drive out from Rapid City we look ahead for the soaring red and lavender rock spires shown in tourist brochures, hoping to see them lifting up from the horizon to relieve the oppressive flatlands monotony. Then we realize that the Badlands don't rise up from the landscape, they drop off from it—an eroded netherworld of grotesquely beautiful forms glowing somberly in the quick-changing light; at sundown they are a rage of shifting primal colors, from palest saffron-yellow to blood-streaked orange to foreboding scarlet-red. ✣ We're looking for Mathew King, a well-known Traditionalist spokesman of the Lakota people. ("Don't call us Sioux," we are repeatedly admonished. "That's White Man's name for us. We are Lakota.") We finally reach the little reservation community of Kyle—a school, a couple of stores, a cafe, a crossroads of intersecting blacktops that quickly become dirt, and a cluster of crumbling government-built houses. A neighbor's gaunt-ribbed dog snarls menacingly but keeps a cautious distance as we knock on Mathew King's screen door. ✣ The short, white-haired, almost impish man before us grins in welcome. "Come on in." He leads us through the kitchen into the living room, sparsely but warmly furnished, and motions for us to sit down on a well-worn couch. He sits down in a chair directly across from us. Though the room is dim, Mathew's smile radiates its own illumination. ✣ The wall behind him is peppered with small holes. "Goons from the Tribal Council did that," he says, shrugging his shoulders. "They accused me of protecting the AIM people, so they shot up the house. Used a shotgun, right through the window. My granddaughter was laying right there on the couch where you're sitting. I didn't do nothing. They never investigated it. But we know who they are. Later on those guys got beaten up pretty bad, but we didn't kill them. I told our boys, 'Don't kill them.' I don't believe in violence. But if I take my guns I can do a lot of damage. I'm an Indian warrior. I'll fight till they kill me!" ✦ He waves his hand when we try to explain why we're here. "I know why you're here! White Man came to this country and forgot his original Instructions. We have never forgotten our Instructions. So you're here looking for the Instructions you lost. I can't tell you what those were, but maybe there are some things I can explain.

It's time Indians tell the world what we know...about nature and about God. So I'm going to tell you what I know and who I am. You guys better listen. You got a lot to learn."

He leans forward in his chair and looks into us, right through us.

WHO I AM

"I'm an Indian. I'm one of God's children. My Indian name is
Noble Red Man. That was my grandfather's name. I'm a
chief. I say what I have to say. That's my duty. If I don't say it,
who's going to say it for me?

I'm a prophet of the Indian people. I can see what's coming. I
prophesy what's going to happen. I can look right into your eyes and
heart and see if you're lying or trying to cheat. I can see if you mean
harm to the Indian people." ✤ "Call me a chief of the Lakota. I'm
a speaker for the chiefs. I walk with the Great Spirit, with God. I
talk to Him. The Great Spirit guides me in my life. Sometimes He
comes to me and tells me what to say. Other times I just speak for
myself, for Mathew King."

THE POWER OF THE PIPE

"I've got Red Cloud's peace pipe. They gave me that when they made
me a chief. I wouldn't accept it in the beginning. He's a great man.
He made all those treaties. He fought when he had to and beat the
White Man's soldiers. Wiped Custer out. He had a lot of powers.

But I'd rather solve my problems through peace. I also have Black Bear's pipe and Noble Red Man's. The Peace Pipe is our only weapon. It's our holy power. It's God's power. The Pipe mediates between man and God. To receive the Pipe, to receive God's gift, you've got to be pure in your heart, mind, body, and soul. And never forget that after the prayers you've got to live that life, a life with God. That's the hardest part."

GOD MADE EVERYTHING SO SIMPLE

"God made everything so simple. Our lives are very simple. We do what we please. The only law we obey is the natural law, God's law. We abide only by that. We don't need your church. We have the Black Hills for our church. And we don't need your Bible. We have the wind and the rain and the stars for our Bible. The world is an open Bible for us. We Indians have studied it for millions and millions of years.

We've learned that God rules the universe and that everything God made is living. Even the rocks are alive. When we use them in our sweat ceremony we talk to them and they talk back to us."

HOW TO TALK TO GOD

"When we want wisdom we go up on the hill and talk to God. Four days and four nights, without food and water. Yes, you can talk to God up on a hill by yourself. You can say anything you want. Nobody's there to listen to you. That's between you and God and nobody else. It's a great feeling to be talking to God. I know. I did it way up on the mountain. The wind was blowing. It was dark. It was cold. And I stood there and I talked to God."

GOD'S MEDICINE

"Once, while I was up on the mountain, I prayed to God to give us a cure for diabetes. And while I was there, somebody said, 'Turn around!' So I turned around and there was the most beautiful Indian woman I'd ever seen. She had long black hair and the most wonderful face. She was holding something out to me in her hand. It was those little berries of the cedar, the dark blue berries on cedar trees. She held them out, but before I could reach out my hand she disappeared." ✤ "I know who she was. She's the one who brought the sacred Pipe to our people. We call her White Buffalo Calf Woman. God sent her to save the Indian people. That was long ago. At that time we were starving, the children were crying. Our hunters circled far and wide to hunt the buffalo and the wild game, but there was nothing, not even a rabbit, not even a bird. We were being punished for having strayed from God, for not knowing Him. His wrath was on us. But still God loved us. He wanted to give His Indian children the Pipe so we could talk and pray with Him whenever we wanted. So He sent that beautiful White Buffalo Calf Woman to us with the Pipe. She took the bundle with the Pipe on her back and set off to carry it to the Indian people. But on her way she met two warriors. She set her bundle down and looked at them. They saw how beautiful she was. Man, you can't resist a woman like that! No man is strong enough to resist a woman. You just can't do it!" ✤ "Well, the first warrior was so afraid when he saw her that he just fell down, too scared to move. But the other warrior right away had evil thoughts about that woman because she was so pretty. So she called the one with the wicked mind over to her and a cloud engulfed him, and when the cloud went away he just lay there, skin and bones, dead. God don't want no evil thoughts!" ✤ "So I knew when I saw her up on the mountain that this was the same woman. But she disappeared before I could take those blue berries from her hand. Later on, when I got diabetes, I forgot about the berries. They sent me to White Man's doctors. They gave me pills. Every morning I had to take insulin. I spent a lot of time in the hospital. Then I remembered White Buffalo Calf Woman and those little blue cedar berries. I picked some, boiled them, strained the juice, and drank it. It's so bitter it took the sugar right out of my body. The doctors checked me and were amazed. They said the diabetes was gone. I didn't have to take insulin anymore. They asked me how I did it, but I didn't say. God gave us medicine to share with people, but if the White Man gets his hands on it he'll charge you a great price and will let you die if you don't have it. God's medicine is free.

God doesn't charge a fee. We don't give money to God. We give Him our prayers, our thanks. And sometimes we give Him the only thing that's really ours: our flesh, our pain. That's what the Sun Dance is all about—giving God our flesh, our pain, and—never forget—a prayer of thanks."

WHITE MAN GETS EVERYTHING WRONG

"He says we're warlike when we're peaceful. He calls us savages, but he's the savage. See, he calls this headdress a warbonnet. Sure, we used it in war, but most of the time it was for ceremony, not war. Each feather stands for a good deed and I have thirty-six in mine. It's not about war; it's about who we are. When we sing songs he calls them war songs. But they're not war songs, they're prayers to God. We have drums, so White Man calls them war drums; but they're not for war, they're for talking to God. There's no such thing as a war drum. He sees how our warriors paint their faces, so he calls it war paint. But it's not for war, it's to make it so God can see our faces clearly if we have to die. So how can we talk to the White Man of peace when he only knows war?"

INDIAN RELIGION

"Indian religion is as old as the Creator. In our way of life the Elders give spiritual direction. The wisdom of thousands of years flows through their lips. Others want to learn what our Elders know. They find some carnival chief who'll give them a sweat bath for $250, and then they think they know all about Indian religion. But you don't sell the religion of your people. Our ceremonies and our religion are not for sale. And we're not selling the Black Hills either."

THE BLACK HILLS

"The White Man wants us to take a hundred million dollars for our Black Hills. But a hundred *billion* wouldn't be enough. Not *four hundred billion!* That wouldn't even pay for the damages you've done. You can never pay us for what you've stolen and destroyed. You can never pay for all the eagles you've killed, for all the buffalo, all the wild game. No, and you can never pay us for all the Indians you've killed. The Black Hills aren't for sale. The Black Hills are where we came out of the earth, where our ancestors are buried, where we go for sacred ceremony. They are the birthplace of the Lakota people. What if we offered you a hundred million dollars for the Vatican?" ✚ "You think it's an accident that you drove us back into these hills and badlands only to find that this land was rich with gold and copper and coal and uranium? Now you want the uranium. But you can't have it. We are the guardians of the uranium of Grandmother Earth. You can't have it. You'll only use it to destroy God's world."

YOU HAVE NEVER THANKED US

"You have taken everything and given us nothing, but worst of all you have never thanked us!" ✚ "You've got to change your ways. I don't have to change. You're the ones who have to change! I live by God's power and I do what He wants me to do. We Indians lived a good life, a happy life until *you* came here and made it miserable. Who gave *you* the right to do that? *You* killed our people. *You* killed our chiefs. *You* stole our land. But God gave us this land. *You* can't take it away!" ✚ Mathew rises from his chair. There's fire in his eyes. His words burn and smoke like brimstone. When he spits out *you,* he doesn't mean some abstract White Man; he means the two of *us* here before him. *We* are the oppressors, the destroyers, the murderers. *We* are the enemy!

GOD'S WRATH: A PROPHECY

"I prophesy many things that come to pass. God is going to put a judgment on the world. He's mad. I'm sorry it's going to happen. He's not going to destroy the whole world. But every living thing will perish, and it'll be maybe another million years before a new life begins again. Grandmother Earth will be alone. She's going to rest. All because of White Man's wickedness. You're going to fall and fall hard. You're going to be crying and wailing. You'll realize you can't get away with destroying God's world. Don't think you can get away with it. God's going to wipe the wickedness from the earth. You can see His signs. Out on the West Coast, Mount St. Helens volcano—that's a sign. And there's going to be earthquakes; maybe half of California and half of Washington and Oregon will go into the water. The same in the East, and in the South. You're going to have volcanoes and earthquakes and hurricanes." ✤ Mathew stood before us, waving his arms like two great eagle wings tossing up tempests below. "It's God giving signs to the White Man, punishing him for not paying his debt to the Indian people, for destroying the land with his greed. And it will get worse until you pay us what you owe us, what you promised us…until you give us what is ours." ✤ "You are going to learn the most important lesson—that God is the most powerful thing there is. We Indians aren't afraid to die. We've got a place to go, a better place, so we don't care. We're ready. We just want you to know. Maybe you can change, maybe you can stop what's coming. There's not much time. It's going to happen. Take it from me. Tell them Noble Red Man said so!"

A BLESSING

Mathew smiles again and suddenly light seems to fill the room. The brimstone settles. He laughs. "Don't worry. You guys still got time to do what you're doing. God's making use of you. He's sending you out to reveal the life of the Indian people. That's a good thing. You should be grateful He's found a use for you." ✤ He seems pleased when we ask for his blessing. "Put your camera on that chair, and, you, put your pen beside it. I'll put a blessing on them so you don't do any harm with them to the Indian people." For several minutes, holding his hands over the camera and pen, he prays in the Lakota language. At one point he stops speaking and holds his head up, as if listening. Standing there beside him as he prays, we can feel the spirit flowing through us like a wind. "I told God what you're doing," Mathew says. "He tells me you're going to have a good journey. No harm will come to the Indian people from what you're doing and no harm will come to you while you're doing it. I asked Him to bless these two men and take care of them."

Since our conversations in 1983, Mathew King—Chief Noble Red Man—has gone on to his Creator. His passing brings to mind these words he spoke to us back then: "You know, last night I had a dream of my wife for the first time since she passed away four years ago. She came to me last night and she told me it's very peaceful up there. It's the best place, far from the wicked world. 'We lead a good life up here,' she said. She wanted me to hurry up and come on up there. So I told her, 'Wait a minute. I got a lot of things to do yet in the world. You better wait a little longer, then I'll be there.' "

CORBETT SUNDOWN ✤ Seneca

A RECOLLECTION BY STEVE WALL

I was looking forward to seeing Chief Corbett Sundown again as we drove up to the Tonawanda Indian reservation in upstate New York, an hour's drive from Buffalo. Three years had passed since our last visit in 1986. At that time, he'd been recuperating from three heart attacks over the previous year and a half. Yet he'd seemed not only alert but feisty and energetic as ever. Here was a man intimately in tune with the Creator, a man who had devoted most of his 80 years to helping his people without thought of recompense. It was simply his duty, and nothing could come in the way of that. Though the heart attacks had forced him to give up his official role as spokesman for the "spiritual fire" of the traditional Six Nations Iroquois, he had continued to function as a leader in Longhouse ceremonies and as a font of wisdom—both practical and spiritual—for those who came to his door. ✤ As Harvey and I drove up to his house at Tonawanda, we saw someone sitting in a parked car in the front driveway. It was Corbett. We walked over to shake his hand, which he extended uncertainly. It was trembling slightly. He didn't remember us at first, but gradually a smile of recognition—weak but genuine—spread across his face. Yet his voice could hardly be heard, a halting whisper, scratchy as an antique phonograph record. We could barely make out the words. ✤ "I like to sit...out here in the car," he said. "Can't walk much anymore. Can't...do nothin'

anymore. Can't..." The words just faded out. His eyes drifted away from us, absorbed in some inner vision. After a minute or so he regathered enough strength to go on: ✤ "I sit out here...I watch things that move," he said. "Yesterday I saw fourteen dogs in the morning. No one else saw'm. I think I know who they are." ✤ "Who are they?" I asked. He didn't answer. His eyes closed. We thought he might have fallen asleep, but he was only looking deep inside himself, trying to find the words, trying to get them out from his mind to his tongue. He didn't mention the dogs again. ✤ "Things come into me," he said at last. "The falling leaves...the stars...I watch them move...they come into me." Once again he lapsed into seeming sleep for a couple of minutes. Then he opened his eyes again. "I'm eighty years old now. I've been a chief for fifty years.." The words trailed off. ✤ We helped him out of the car

and into the house, where two lovely ladies—Edna Parker, 85, and
Betsy Carpenter, 96—tend to his care. "They think I'm a little boy,"
he said, smiling. He sat down at the cluttered kitchen table where
we'd had so many wonderful conversations in the past. But there
would be no conversation this day. Every so often his eyes bright-
ened, as if with some thought, and his lips would begin to move—but
only a hoarse sigh came out. ✤ I realized that whatever Corbett
had to say to us had already been said. There would be no more. He
began slowly to clench and unclench his hands, holding them out in
front of him and squinting at them as if they were miles away.

"Can't...can't feel my hands," he whispered. ✤ Something came into me, a sudden impulse. I walked over to him and took his two hands in mine. They were cool, dry, like cracked leather. They felt barely alive. Like a mother rubbing her child's frozen hands, I pressed and squeezed and rubbed them gently, praying that some of the life and warmth might flow from my hands into his. "These are powerful hands, Corbett," I told him. "These are hands that have led their people well." ✤ Corbett's eyes welled with tears. I could not restrain my own. His lips moved silently, trying to deliver the words so far back in his mind. Only a sound like faint static came out. ✤ "Corbett," I asked, "May I photograph your hands?" With Edna's and Betsy's help we took him back out of doors into the light. He sat in a lawn chair. For ten minutes, focusing through my tears, I photographed those magnificent hands. Somehow they had ceased trembling. Their strength—no, call it power—is something I will never forget. When I'd finished, I took them once more in mine. ✤ Corbett sat there, looking up at me. His tears had dried and his quiet smile said everything words could not. Words? We had come for the gift of his words. There was so much we wanted to hear, so much he could tell us. But words were something irrelevant now. A deeper communication was taking place. He had given us the blessing of his presence, and no greater gift can be imagined.

HARRIETT STARLEAF GUMBS ✤
Shinnecock

Tucked away just west of the posh Hamptons, the Shinnecock Indian Reservation—hardly noticeable from the road—occupies one of the last pieces of unspoiled shoreside real estate on eastern Long Island. Only the quick-glancing tourist sees the hand-lettered sign on a one-story wooden building: "Shinnecock Indian Outpost & Starleaf's Antique Bottle Shop." Starleaf is the Indian name of Harriett Gumbs, a youngish Elder of her people, a tribal spokeswoman, teacher, and historian. ✤ "We were here for thousands and thousands of years before the first white settlers arrived in 1640," she tells us as we stroll the rock- and shell-strewn shore of Shinnecock Bay on a chilly, somberly beautiful early December afternoon. From this same shore came the purple-shelled clam called the quahog, from which the Indians of the Northeast once made the purple beads for their sacred wampum. "Our ancestors called this place 'Sea-wan-hac-hee', or 'Shell-Heaven', " Starleaf says. "Back then the land was ours for miles around. Now we have only these 400 acres. They've taken all the rest. Some developers recently offered us millions to relocate, but we refused. This land is ours forever—and we're not leaving." ✤ She retells a story told to her by her great-grandmother, Elizabeth Adams, who lived to be over a hundred years old.

THE ORIGIN OF OUR PEOPLE

"A beautiful dove flew over the earth and dropped a bit of blood from its wounded wing onto Mother Nature's warm breast. Many Indians believed this might be so, for the trees sang softly and their branches swayed gracefully up and down in the gentle winds, fanning the spot where the blood had landed.

A bit of sunshine, a drop of rain, a puff of life from the Great Spirit as He gently breathed upon that spot, created the Native Americans. They were well-formed and agile, copper-colored and proud."

Starleaf sighs. "Today we need a revolution to survive. So much has been taken, so much has been lost. We hardly know our own language or culture anymore. That was taken from us—along with the land and, yes, even the sea and the streams. When I was a girl the water was so clean and clear we bathed and washed our clothes in it. Now there's so much pollution no one wants to set foot in it." ✤

"What a difference between White Man's way and the Indian way!

44

We lived here since time began and the only waste we left behind was the oyster-shell middens on the shore. But what will future archaeologists find when they unearth today's civilization? Generations to come will look back and see how 20th-century Americans were the garbage-makers, the poison-producers, the carcinogen-creators." ✤ "In exchange for all he's taken from us, all White Man gives us back is 'welfare', and even for that little bit he forces our men to leave their homes so their children can get food to eat. That's rape—raping someone's way of life, raping someone's culture and heritage, raping the land and raping the sea. What kind of legacy is that? We reject it. We want no part of it.

We only ask to survive so that we can remain who and what we are—and for that we will always thank the Creator. We ask only the chance to pass on our way of life and our love for the Creator to our children and grandchildren."

SHORESIDE FEAST OF THANKSGIVING

Starleaf arranges a traditional feast on the beach, supervised by her son Phil Brown, a professional chef. Two days are spent gathering and preparing the victuals—a veritable cornucopia of fresh-caught foods from the Bay and its shore: steamed clams and crabs, oysters raw and grilled, baked mussels, stuffed scallops, thick clam chowder, exquisite deep-baked bluefish, plus tidbits of rabbit, squirrel, duck, and venison. ✤ For appetizers we dig fresh clams from the wet sand, pry them open, and simply pop them into our mouths. "You don't need lemon or hot sauce," Starleaf says. "They're perfect the way they are, the way the Creator made them." She recalls:

"There used to be so many clams on the beach you only had to kick the sand to find them. You could dig them up with your toes. Now they're scarce. Commercial clammers rake the shore right up to the tideline. When I was a girl the sand was pearly white. Now it's covered with that green algae—from pollution, they say. The pesticides and herbicides and fertilizers run down from the potato fields. Still, isn't it beautiful? This is where the Creator intended us to live." ✤ After hours of preparation, Phil announces that the feast is ready, and we gather around the pit-fire on the beach at dusk. The air is a symphony of savors. "But first," Starleaf says, "let's join hands and pray." For this grand occasion she's donned a traditional Indian costume of skins, an embroidered shawl, and elegant beadwork. She exudes a gentle majesty and unpretentious spirituality. As we raise our joined hands in the air and lift our faces to the sky, she intones:

"We give thanks to the Creator
for these fruits of the sea.
We ask his blessings on the food that we eat
and on all the generations that follow us
down to the Seventh Generation.
May the world we leave them be a better one
than was left to us.

Amen."

EDDIE BENTON-BANAI ✤ Ojibway

We seek out this extraordinary educator one Monday morning in 1984 at the Red School House, his alternative Indian school in St. Paul, housed in a turn-of-the-century brick building that was formerly a Roman Catholic parochial school. Over the main door the original lintel reads: "Suffer ye the little children to come unto me." Here, each Monday morning, the week begins with a prayer. Already the sacred water drum—"The Little Boy," as the Ojibway lovingly call him—is beating within, pounding out an ancient rhythm that beats directly on the heart. The whole building is a beating heart at this moment. We are ushered into a large open classroom and stand at the edge of several concentric circles of children and teachers, some seated, some standing, some sitting cross-legged on the floor. At the center of the room, three teenage boys and a man—Eddie Benton-Banai himself—are flailing away at the drum, and the Voice of the Little Boy fills the Universe. ✤ Here the Creator is being honored and all else ceases. The sacred fire—a small version of it—has been lit in a ceremonial vessel at the center of the first-floor classroom. The aromas of sage and sweetgrass are dazzlingly pungent; the smoke from the fire and tobacco offerings momentarily grows thick, and the large school-windows are thrown open. Fingers of smoke rush outward, carrying the prayers up to the Creator, who must be listening hard, His ear pressed close to the open windows of His beloved Red School House. ✤ Still in the robust vigor of middle life, yet nonetheless an authentic Wisdomkeeper, Eddie Benton-Banai is a founder of the American Indian Movement and of the Red School House; he's also a Midewiwin priest, philosopher, poet—and one-time coach of the Red School House football team. His life's mission is simple: the education of his people. After leaving the Red School House, he has continued as a professional educational consultant and also serves as the Grand Chief of the Three Fires Society. ✤ "We have to pick up things our people have left along the trail," Eddie tells us. "Everything wasn't passed down. Too many of our people died too quick back then. They didn't have time to pass it all down. So we Indians today have to go back and find the things that got left along the trail. It's up to us to go back and pick them up. We have to educate ourselves to know who we are. That's what I mean when I say, 'Teach the children.' The Grandfathers and the Grandmothers are in the children. If we educate them right, our children tomorrow will be wiser than we are today. They're the Grandfathers and Grandmothers of tomorrow. That's what the Red School House is all about." ✤ "My life belongs to my people. That makes me a very busy man. I may not always have the time to look after you or talk to you. But you guys hang around if you like. Maybe you'll learn something. There's only one price I ask you to pay—and, I'm sorry, but it's a very high price. I ask you to pay the price of attention!"

THE SPIRITUAL FIRE STILL BURNS

"The spiritual heritage of Native American people is here—it has not been extinguished. I believe the spiritual fire still burns and is beckoning for America, indeed, the world, to come closer, to listen, to learn, and to share in its warmth and comfort.

I, as a spiritual Indian man, am convinced that it is time to reach out to my white brothers and sisters and to share with whomever wishes to partake of what we, the indigenous people of this land, still have. It is time that the buckskin curtain be drawn back. It is time, I know it."

A RENAISSANCE IS TAKING PLACE

"A renaissance is taking place among Native American peoples. This renaissance is not of a material nature. It is a spiritual renaissance, a retrieving and reviving of our original covenant with the Creator. We are reaffirming our relationship and stewardship with our Mother the Earth. While we are inspired and directed to do this for our children and ourselves, we also realize that many, not all, of our Elders have fallen asleep, forgotten, or have never known our rightful spiritual heritage. Therefore, it is up to those of us who have, in whatever measure, the teachings, philosophy, and traditions, including the rituals, to work for their revival and continuance."

WHAT IS SOVEREIGNTY?

"Personally I'm sovereign. I'm not dependent on anybody. For thirteen years I was a high-steel construction man. I did that very well and I loved it. It satisfied something in my ego and my manhood. But then, after I'd put up hundreds of towers and skyscrapers and bridges, I looked around and saw that no skyscrapers were being built on the reservation. I said, 'Hey, this ain't doin' my people any good.' So I climbed down off the iron and picked up the flag of self-determination. Then I had to learn how to make my family sovereign, how to make my people sovereign. Sovereignty is something that goes in ever-widening circles, beginning with yourself. In order for Indian people to attain sovereignty, each of us has to be sovereign in ourselves. If a person can go out into the stream and fish for their needs, if they can do whatever they have to do to provide for those who are dependent on them, then that person is sovereign. Sovereignty isn't something someone gives you. You can't give us our sovereignty. Sovereignty isn't a privilege someone gives you. It's a responsibility you carry inside yourself. In order for my people to achieve sovereignty, each man and woman among us has to be sovereign. Sovereignty begins with yourself."

GROWING UP RED

"I am a full-blood Indian man. My real name is Bawdway Wi Dun: It means 'Messenger' and is derived from the Thunder Beings. I was born in a wigwam by natural childbirth and raised in total Ojibway traditional manner. I was given many of the old traditional and spiritual teachings and rituals pure, first hand. I began fasting at age five, and fasted at ages seven, nine, eleven, and thirteen. I didn't begin speaking English until age ten. I was chosen, prepared, and taught to be a Midewiwin teacher. Currently I hold a fourth-degree priesthood in the Midewiwin Lodge of the Ojibway people. The fourth degree is the priesthood level of our religious order and belief. I am also a keeper and carrier of the sacred water drum and the Pipe of everlasting prayer. But do not call me an 'Elder'—that is an honor I have yet to earn from my people. I am but a teacher and a believer." ✚ "My mother was a healer, and so she had to move around the country a great deal gathering roots and herbs and all of the other things for her pharmacy. My father was a lumberjack, a trapper, a slave-laborer, a railroad-track laborer. I remember, almost from the time I could walk, we would pick rutabagas and potatoes for a penny or two a bag at a farmer's place. We had to walk maybe ten miles to get there, worked all day, got our few pennies, then walked back home. My father would use the money to buy some food for the family. Then next morning we went out again to pick more rutabagas and potatoes. That's how my family provided for us. By today's standards it may seem a hard life. But I thought I had a wonderful home. It was warm. Everyone there spoke to one another and it was in our own language, the only language that was spoken there. Everyone in that wigwam loved each other. So I come from a very, very rich home and I'm proud of it." ✚ "I spent a good part of my life in the white world. I was forced to go to a BIA boarding school and also to a Catholic mission school. I don't know which of those schools I remember more fondly. At the Catholic mission school we were made to sit in a room, all facing towards the front, and the good kind loving sister stood up there and she taught whatever it was she was teaching us. I hardly ever understood. When it came time to answer questions, she would say, 'Edward, stand up and tell me, who was the King of Spain in 1492?' And I would stand up and say, 'I don't know.' Only I would say it in Ojibway, not English—for which I was summarily snatched by the ear and marched up in front of the room and told to stretch out my hands, palms down, and the good kind loving sister would hit the backs of my hands twelve times with her yardstick. That was repeated almost daily. I never did learn who the hell the King of Spain was. Maybe I should have. Maybe my little finger would be

straight now." ✚ "One incident I remember rather well. Because I refused to speak English all the time, they decided to make me an altar boy. I thought that was something, that I was really moving up in the world. The only problem, they said, was that I had to learn a language in order to be an altar boy, and the language was Latin. And so I learned some Latin. I didn't know what all those words meant, but with a little effort I could repeat them. To this day I remember all the actions that go with being an altar boy. One reason I wanted to be an altar boy was that every Sunday after Mass you got a bowl of Jell-O with whipped cream on top. Boy, it was good! It was about the only good thing I ever got there." ✚ "And then there was the BIA boarding school. I happened to go to a very endearing institution called the Pipestone Indian Training School. I'll never forget my first day there. We'd been riding on a school bus the better part of that day from Wisconsin to southwestern Minnesota, and we arrived at Pipestone around midnight. I thought for sure they would feed us—but they didn't do that. They marched us all, boys in one direction and girls in the other, and the first stop was this little room that had four chairs in it. And there everybody got their hair lopped off. I remember how I cried. My mother used to take care of my braids and, I remember, when I left her earlier that day, she had tied an eagle plume in my hair. She said, 'I want you to look nice when you get there.' She also told me, 'Always remember to take care of your hair. Braid it when you can but for sure keep it clean, comb it, tie it back. But always remember, when you go out to pray your hair must be in braids. And I want you to keep this eagle plume with you until we get back together.' That same night they chopped off my hair. And I mean they cut it right down to the skin. And there on the floor lay my pretty eagle plume and the braids that my mother had so carefully fixed and tied. That was the first atrocity I experienced at the BIA boarding school. From that room we were marched into a shower—a big, long, common shower—and some kind of substance was poured all over us to 'delouse' us, they said. That was the second atrocity. Then all of our clothes were taken away from us and we were all dressed in blue coveralls. If we were wearing moccasins, those were taken away and we were all put into government-issue black shoes. So that was my first day at the BIA boarding school, and I shall always remember that. I will let you guess which one of those boarding schools I loved the best."

Vernon Cooper ✤ Lumbee

Head west out of Lumberton, North Carolina, cross the Lumber River, and you enter the territory of the Lumbee—the largest Indian tribe east of the Mississippi and one of the least known. Lacking either a reservation or official federal recognition, some 35,000 Lumbee—formerly known as the Croatoan tribe—cling tenaciously to ancestral lands in rural Robeson County, which they share, at times uneasily, with 40,000 whites and 25,000 blacks. ✤ Historians theorize that the Lumbee's ancestors absorbed the missing white settlers of the famous "Lost Colony" founded by Sir Walter Raleigh on the Virginia coast in the 1580s. (The only clue to the colonists' disappearance was the word "Croatoan" carved on a tree.) When Europeans moved into North Carolina's deep interior in the 1700s, they found an English-speaking tribe of Indians, often fair-skinned and blue-eyed, who practiced their own form of Christianity. Apparently, having fled the encroaching white settlers on the Virginia and North Carolina coasts, the ancestors of today's Lumbee sought refuge in the dark, foreboding swamps along the

Lumber River. ✤ Vernon Cooper, 84 on our first visit in 1989, is a direct link to those events of four centuries ago. "My grandmother passed the healing power on to me from her deathbed in 1917," he tells us. "She said this ability was a gift that had been given to our family for four hundred years. She told me, 'You will be the last one with that gift in our family. There will never be another one. You'll finish out the four hundred years.' When my daughter was born I prayed the prophecy would be changed, that she could become a healer, too. But it wasn't to be. There's a few others here who work with herbs. I've passed on what I could. But the gift of healing with your hands—that can't be passed on. I only wish I could."

ON HEALING

"There's nothing happens to a person that can't be cured if you get what it takes to do it. We come out of the earth, and there's something in the earth to cure everything. In the old days, before my time, it took only a single herb to cure a person; now it takes a combination. Trouble is, you can't find most of the herbs and roots around here anymore. All those farm chemicals have killed'm off. You've got to go up in the hills to find them, and I'm getting too old for that anymore.

Everything I know I learned by listening and watching. Nowadays people learn out of books instead. Doctors study what man has learned. I pray to understand what man has forgotten.

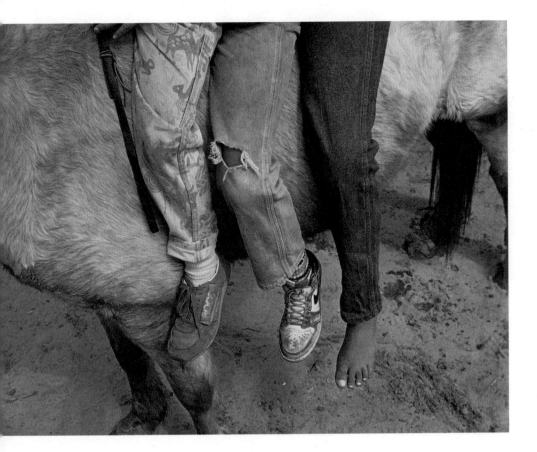

I don't fix a tonic until I'm sure what's wrong with a person. I don't make guesses. I have to be sure, because medicine can do bad as well as good, and I don't want to hurt anybody. Whatever the Lord shows me that's what I'm going to do. Maybe it takes some herbs. Maybe it takes some touching. But most of all it takes faith." ✚

"The gift my grandmother passed on is diagnosing and healing by touch, by laying on of hands. We call it 'rubbing.' I rub people with my hands to find the sickness. I pray to the Lord for help. If the patient has faith, the fever'll come right out, right into my hands. I can feel the heat in my fingers. Sometimes the skin peels right off my hands. I can feel the patient's pain like an electric shock. My

veins swell up for days. Feel this lump in my hand? I got that from a man I treated. Came right out of his hand into mine. I asked the Lord to let me have it. It never went away. You got to be careful with these things. There's no heavier burden than being a healer." ✤ "Sometimes I get real tired. I work all night, night after night. One patient after another. Maybe I get to bed at one or two in the morning. Then, at five, someone's knocking on my door and it starts all over. That's the way it was for years, though I'm slowing down now. People asked me why I didn't take a vacation so I could get over being tired. But I tell'm I don't want any vacation. If I got rested up, why, I'd just start working even harder and get tired all over again. So I'd just as soon stay tired." ✤ "I haven't got time for vacations. I've not finished my work in this world yet. Vacations would only delay my time of reaching that wondrous land I'm going to. It won't be long now. So I'm going to finish what the Lord put me here to do. Then, when I go to that other place, I'll be able to rest and never be interrupted again. I can tell you, I'm looking forward to that."

THE AGE WE'RE LIVING IN

"I just wasn't cut out for the age we're living in. Everybody's hurrying but nobody's going anywhere. People aren't living, they're only existing. They're growing away from spiritual realities.

> These days people seek knowledge, not wisdom. Knowledge is of the past; wisdom is of the future.

We're in an age now when people are slumbering. They think they're awake, yet they're really sleeping. But this is a dangerous age, the most dangerous in human history. People need to wake up. They can't hear God's voice if they're asleep." ✠ "Heavy equipment and light-minded people have destroyed just about everything nature has provided. Well, we can't keep ruining the earth and poisoning it and think we can get away with it. Certain destruction is going to hit one of these days. We're on the verge of a change such as has never been before. God is going to intervene."

"I'm tired now," Vernon says. "Been feeling poorly lately. Haven't been able to gather any herbs since Thanksgiving last year. I've been even more tired than usual. Maybe I'll get that long-awaited rest pretty soon. Anyway, you come back another time, if you like. I'm always glad to work with anyone looking for the betterment of the coming generation." ✠ "But you fellows see you write it all down right. If you write it wrong, people'll believe it wrong."

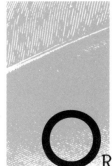

O REN LYONS ✛ Onondaga

A stern-faced Oren Lyons, Faithkeeper of the Turtle Clan of the Onondaga Nation and spokesman for the Six Nations Iroquois Confederacy, sits across a wooden table from us in his log cabin on the Onondaga reservation a few miles south of Syracuse, New York. It's night and the harsh light of a single kerosene lantern casts sharp shadows against the walls and beamed ceiling. ✛ "I prefer no electricity," Oren says. "And no phones. That's important!" In one corner, shrouded in shadow, hangs an assemblage of ceremonial masks, faces turned to the wall. "We show their faces only during ceremonies. And we never allow photographs of our ceremonies, so don't even think of asking." He gives us a long, hard look and shakes his head. "Why come to us? We're the toughest nut to crack. You think we turn our Elders over to anyone who walks in the door? He leans forward, elbows planted on the table. His eyes probe us. "We guard them like pure spring water. "So what is it you guys want from the Elders?" Oren asks. "Secrets? Mystery?" ✛ We explain that we want only to meet them and hear whatever they care to share with us, that we're not looking for secrets. "That's good," Oren says, "because,

I can tell you right now, there are no secrets. There's no mystery. There's only common sense."

He gets up, strides over to the cast-iron stove, and warms his hands. Outside, a cold January wind is moaning, pelting the windows with

dry icy snow. We sit uneasily, sure he's about to send us packing into that bitter night. Still rubbing his hands, he sits down and faces us. "Common sense...," he says, picking up the echo of his own words. "I'll tell you guys a little bit about common sense..."

THE NATURAL LAW

"What law are you living under? United States government law? That's Man's law. You break Man's law and you pay a fine or go to jail—maybe. That's the way it is with Man's law. You can break it and still get around it. Maybe you won't get punished at all. Happens all the time. People figure they can get away with anything and half the time they do. But they forget there's another law, the Creator's law. We call it Natural Law . . . Natural law prevails everywhere. It supersedes Man's law. If you violate it, you get hit. There's no judge and jury, there's no lawyers or courts, you can't buy or dodge or beg your way out of it. If you violate this Natural law you're going to get hit and get hit hard.

One of the Natural laws is that you've got to keep things pure. Especially the water. Keeping the water pure is one of the first laws of life. If you destroy the water, you destroy life.

That's what I mean about common sense. Anybody can see that. All life on Mother Earth depends on the pure water, yet we spill every kind of dirt and filth and poison into it. That makes no common sense at all. Your legislature can pass a law saying it's OK, but it's not OK. Natural law doesn't care about your Man's law. Natural law's going to hit you. You can't get out of the way. You don't fool around with Natural law and get away with it. If you kill the water, you kill the life that depends on it, your own included. That's Natural law. It's also common sense."

ALL LIFE IS EQUAL

"Another of the Natural laws is that all life is equal. That's our philosophy. You have to respect life—all life, not just your own. The key word is 'respect.' Unless you respect the earth, you destroy it. Unless you respect all life as much as your own life, you become a destroyer, a murderer.

Man sometimes thinks he's been elevated to be the controller, the ruler. But he's not. He's only a part of the whole. Man's job is not to exploit but to oversee, to be a steward. Man has responsibility, not power."

THE SEVENTH GENERATION

"In our way of life, in our government, with every decision we make, we always keep in mind the Seventh Generation to come. It's our job to see that the people coming ahead, the generations still unborn, have a world no worse than ours—and hopefully better. When we walk upon Mother Earth we always plant our feet carefully because we know the faces of our future generations are looking up at us from beneath the ground. We never forget them." Oren slips off into the shadows of the cabin and returns with a beaded wampum belt about four inches wide and a foot and half long.

THE TWO ROW WAMPUM

"This is a replica of the Two Row Wampum, the basis of our sovereignty. It's the Grandfather of all the treaties between our two peoples. We made it with the Dutch in the early 1600s. The two rows of purple beads represent the Red Man and the White Man living side by side in peace and friendship forever. The white background is a river. On that river of life you travel in your boat and we travel in our canoe. Each of us is responsible for our own government and religion and way of life. We don't interfere with each other. The rows are parallel. One row is not bigger. We're equal. We don't call each other 'Father' or 'Son', we call each other 'Brother.' That's the way it's supposed to be between us

'for as long as the grass grows and water flows and the sun shines.' Those words come from this treaty. We still believe them. We're waiting for the White Man to live up to his side.

Right now he's hogging the middle of the river and pushing us aside. But we remember how it's supposed to be, how we agreed in the beginning when you were weak and we were strong. White Man seems to have forgotten. But we've got a long memory. And so has the Creator . . . Our ancestors told us that there will come a time in the future when some of our people will put one foot in the canoe and one in the boat. That's a very precarious position to be in. And they foretold a great wind would rise that would tear the canoe and boat away from each other. Then those people who have one foot in the canoe and one foot in the boat are going to fall into this river. And no power this side of the Creation can save them."

WE ARE THE HAUDENOSAUNEE

"We are the Haudenosaunee. That means 'People of the Longhouse.' We are made up of Six Nations. Each of us is equal. Each of us is sovereign. And we come together in a Confederacy. Our business is peace, not war... In issues of peace and war and other major matters we sit together and make our decisions. There is no single authority. We do not vote. We must reach a decision that everyone agrees with. And we have a method by which we arrive at that decision. ✚ We have a Central Fire, and we have three sides to the fire.

Our Elder Brothers, the Seneca and Mohawk, sit on one side of the fire; our Younger Brothers, the Oneida, Cayuga, and Tuscarora, sit on the other side; and in front sit the Onondaga, the keepers of the Central Fire. Each side of the fire has one speaker, and he speaks on behalf of those he sits with. A problem is presented from what we call the Well. From there it goes to each of the sides for discussion. Each side agrees or disagrees among itself and sends its decision on the problem back to the Well. There it is adjusted to conform with the decisions of the others. Then it's sent back out from the Well again. This goes on until the issue is unanimously decided. ✤ This is a very old Indian-style government. It requires complete unity of decision. It takes time. But the decisions, once made, are very firm. If there's a problem we can't seem to resolve, we reconsider it another time. If, after a third time, there's still no unanimous decision, then the Tadodaho, or presiding chief—who comes from the Onondaga, the keepers of the Central Fire—will announce a compromise decision. But if the problem is still divisive, the Tadodaho will say, 'We will not address it at all', because there's no problem that's important enough to cause divisions among the people. ✤ The Peacemaker who founded our Confederacy told us, we must be of one mind. Those are good words to remember today—or any day."

CONSCIOUSNESS

I do not see a delegation
For the Four-footed.
I see no seat for the eagles.

We forget and we consider
Ourselves superior.

But we are after all
A mere part of the Creation.

And we must consider
To understand where we are.

And we stand somewhere between
The mountain and the Ant.

Somewhere and only there
As part and parcel
Of the Creation.

CHIEF OREN LYONS

(From an address to the Non-Governmental Organizations of the
United Nations, Geneva, Switzerland, 1977)

Leila Fisher ✢ Hoh

After a two-hour drive through the misty, darkly beautiful rain forest of Washington State's Olympic Peninsula, we come to the Hoh Indian reservation—a mere 443 acres perched at the edge of the Pacific. Just before the two-lane blacktop gives out onto the beach, we stop and knock at the door of a small frame house. "Come on in!" calls a woman's voice. Within, in the sparsely furnished living room, Hoh Elder Leila Fisher sits in a well-worn armchair, her fingers deftly weaving one of the straw baskets she's noted for. She can't imagine why two strangers would want to talk to her, and she suggests we go out on the beach where a feast and powwow has just begun. Through the open windows we can hear the sound of a far-away drum and distant voices singing. ✢ "They're singing songs of the earth," Leila says. "I'm too weak to go out there with them, but I love hearing the children's voices sing those songs. I helped teach them, you know. They're my children. All children are my children. I teach them the songs and whatever else I can. That's what Grandmothers are for—to teach songs and tell stories and show them the right berries to pick and roots to dig. And also to give them all the love they can stand. No better job in the world than being a Grandmother! Now you boys get out there before the food's all gone—but before you go I'll tell you just one little story. It's one of my favorites—and it's true."

HOW WISDOM COMES

"Did you ever wonder how wisdom comes?" Without taking her
hands from her weaving or even looking up to see if we're listening,
she continues: "There was a man, a postman here on the reservation, who heard some of the Elders talking about receiving objects
that bring great power. He didn't know much about such things, but
he thought to himself that it would be a wonderful thing if he could
receive such an object—which can only be bestowed by the Creator.
In particular, he heard from the Elders that the highest such object
a person can receive is an eagle feather. He decided that was the one
for him. If he could just receive an eagle feather he would have all
the power and wisdom and prestige he desired. But he knew he
couldn't buy one and he couldn't ask anyone to give him one. It just
had to come to him somehow by the Creator's will." ✤ "Day after
day he went around looking for an eagle feather. He figured one
would come his way if he just kept his eyes open. It got so he

thought of nothing else. That eagle feather occupied his thoughts from sunup to sundown. Weeks passed, then months, then years. Every day the postman did his rounds, always looking for that eagle feather—looking just as hard as he could. He paid no attention to his family or friends. He just kept his mind fixed on that eagle feather. But it never seemed to come. He started to grow old, but still no feather. Finally, he came to realize that no matter how hard he looked he was no closer to getting the feather than he had been the day he started." ✤ "One day he took a break by the side of the road. He got out of his little jeep mail-carrier and had a talk with the Creator. He said: 'I'm so tired of looking for that eagle feather. Maybe I'm not supposed to get one. I've spent all my life thinking about that feather. I've hardly given a thought to my family and friends. All I cared about was that feather, and now life has just about passed me by. I've missed out on a lot of good things. Well, I'm giving up the search. I'm going to stop looking for that feather and start living. Maybe I have time enough left to make it up to my family and friends. Forgive me for the way I have conducted my life.'" ✤ "Then—and only then—a great peace came into him. He suddenly felt better inside than he had in all these years. Just as he finished his talk with the Creator and started getting back in his jeep, he was surprised by a shadow passing over him. Holding his hands over his eyes, he looked up into the sky and saw, high above, a great bird flying over. Almost instantly it disappeared. Then he saw something floating down ever so lightly on the breeze—a beautiful tail feather. It was his eagle feather! He realized that the feather had come not a single moment before he had stopped searching and made his peace with the Creator.

> He finally learned that wisdom comes only when you stop looking for it and start truly living the life the Creator intended for you.

That postman is still alive and he's a changed person. People come to him for wisdom now and he shares everything he knows. Even though now he has the power and the prestige he searched for, he no longer cares about such things. He's concerned about others, not himself. So now you know how wisdom comes."

BUFFALO JIM ✚ Seminole

As we leave Alligator Alley and drive up the narrow paved road to the Big Cypress Seminole Indian Reservation we pass a small bullet-riddled sign: "U.S. Government Property, Department of the Interior." The land on either side is brown and grim, a flat and monotonous expanse of nearly dry sawgrass marsh dotted with sparsely treed hummocks—knoll-like remnants of former islands in the now largely drained swamp called Big Cypress, just north of Everglades National Park. ✚ At a small roadside grocery and diner—the only commercial establishment in sight—we stop to ask the way to the home of Buffalo Jim, the aged medicine man we're seeking out. Minutes later we drive up a dirt rut of a road that gives out in a patch of tall brown weeds and ragged undergrowth from which rises a plain rectangular cinderblock house. ✚ We knock. There's an abrupt rustling sound inside, then silence. We have that sense of nervous expectation we invariably get when approaching one of the Grandfathers or Grandmothers for the first time. We know we are about to be measured, and measured hard. ✚ Now the door opens a crack, and there he stands—a bent but still tallish reed of a man with a long face enmeshed in an intricate filigree of deep, leathery wrinkles. Almost all we know of Buffalo Jim is contained in a few faded newspaper clippings from the early 1970s, when he took part in a brief-lived federal program to help young Seminole apprentices in the fast-dying traditional healing arts.

Because he speaks little English, his words must be translated for us from the Mikosukee language by Joe Jumper, Buffalo's understudy in herbal matters for many years. (We would later learn with great sadness of Joe's untimely death in middle age in 1987.) ✚ Widely revered among his people for his herbal knowledge and spiritual powers, Buffalo has practiced medicine for more than seventy years, being especially renowned for his ability to ease pain through the use of sacred curing songs. Of such matters, however, he refuses to speak. "White man always wants to know what he can't understand, what can only hurt him," Buffalo says, "but if you want to talk about other things than medicine and ceremony, come in." ✚ Buffalo—

his first name is Buffalo, his family name is Jim—was born, according to tribal records, on January 11, 1889. That would make him 94 at our first visit in 1983 and 100 at our last in 1989. Buffalo, however, insists he's several years older than that. ✤ The path to his little house is always busy. In a cluttered back room he works up special potions prepared according to ancient formulae. Out back, in the bountiful vegetation of encroaching swamplands, a natural pharmaceutical garden of remedies grows right up to his door. Patients often leave a chicken or ham or slab of beef for payment; he's wearing two watches and five rings—gifts from patients—on our first meeting. He gestures for us to sit down around the kitchen table.

"Ask me questions from your heart," says Buffalo Jim, "and I'll give you answers from my heart."

"We have no particular questions, Buffalo. What would you like to talk about?" ✤ After a deep silence he smiles, chuckling. ✤ "We can talk of birds!" he laughs, flapping his arms as if to fly. He holds up an eagle feather someone has brought for a blessing. "Birds," he says, "have always been important to the Indian because they go where they wish, they light where they may, and they're free. We take these feathers from the birds. We use them in our ceremony because the feathers remind us of the Creator. The eagle flies highest in the sky of all the birds and so he is the nearest to the Creator, and his feather is the most sacred of all. He is the highest of the birds and so belongs to all the tribes, to all the peoples. And then each tribe has a lesser bird of its own. For the Seminole, it's the heron."

TWO SIGNS OF THE END OF THE WORLD

Taking us out to the little open-air palm-thatched chickee outside
his house, Buffalo continues: ✛ "The Creator told us two things
will happen just before the end of the world. The first thing is that
we will lose our language. That will be one of the signs. And
already, you see, the children cannot speak the old language anymore. And the second sign is that we will forget how to make our
sacred fire. No one really knows how to do it anymore. They may
try, but they don't really know if they're doing it the right way, the
way the Creator taught us long ago. I can barely remember how the
Old Ones did it. I was just a boy then in the 1890s. Here, let me see
if I can show you." ✛ To demonstrate how the Old Ones struck the
spark from flint to light the sacred fire, Buffalo takes an aluminum
fork in one hand and a rock from the ground with the other. He lifts
the fork above his head and brings it down sharply against the rock.
He manages only to skin his thumb. Later, we bring a flintstone
from a museum, hoping perhaps he can strike a spark to restart a
symbolic sacred fire. Still something is missing—"the steel piece to
make the spark," he says. He's gotten a bit of dry cypress bark, the
traditional sacred kindling used in Seminole ceremony, and now,

sadly, shrugging his thin shoulders, simply lights it with a match—
an impromptu and improper sacred fire, perhaps, but nonetheless
sacred to those of us standing there. Its brief spurt of living flame
and quick guttering-out bring us back to the subject of the end of
the world.

THE EARTH IS LIKE AN ANIMAL

"The earth is like an animal," Buffalo says. "When an animal is sick
it wiggles and twitches. Just before it dies it shakes even harder,
shakes all over. That's what we call the earthquake and the volcano.
You'll see, it's already starting to happen. The world is wiggling and
twitching and shaking just before it dies."

THE END OF FLORIDA

"The Creator made it so that Florida was shaped like the nose of a
deer. One of these days soon the Creator will break the nose off the
deer. Florida will break off and fall into the sea. Yes, you watch, it
will happen. The time is just about here. Nothing can stop it." ✤
And what will happen to the people of Florida? ✤ He smiles
darkly, rocking slightly in his chair. "All be dead," he says. "All be
dead." Buffalo's dark smile now turns benign and brightens. "Next
we talk of beginnings!"

HOW EARTH WAS CREATED

"In the beginning the world had no land. Only water. The Creator
came down here but there was nowhere to walk. Then He saw a
little bass swimming around down in the water. The bass was tired
of swimming all the time. He wanted to rest. So he started diving
down to the bottom, getting a grain of sand and putting it on a pile
of other grains of sand. After a long time the pile of sand came up
above the surface of the water and the little bass could rest on it.
That gave the Creator an idea, because He was tired of wading
around in the water. So he told the bass: 'You go down again and
bring me up four grains of sand.' And the bass did it. Then the Creator saw a sea cow—a manatee—and He told her: 'Take one of these
grains of sand and hit it with your tail to the West.' So the sea cow hit

the grain of sand with her tail and it rolled out to the West, and where it rolled the land formed behind it, and as the land formed there was thunder and the world shook. Then He told the sea cow: 'Take the second grain of sand and hit it with your tail to the South.' She did it, and again the land formed and the thunder shook. Then she did it with the two other grains of sand, to the North and to the East. That was how the world started."

THE WOODPECKER, THE BUZZARD, & THE RACCOON

"After the Creator made the land, He sent out the woodpecker to take a look. The woodpecker, he flapped his wings up and down, sharp and hard, like this." Buffalo snaps his elbows abruptly up and down. "When he flew over the land his wings hit the ground and that was how the mountains were created." ✤ "The Creator sent the buzzard out for a look, too. The buzzard, he flies flat, with his wings out like this." Buffalo holds his arms out wide, fingers outstretched like wing tips, as if gliding. "Where his wings hit the ground, that was where we had the flatland and the valleys." ✤ "Another animal was the raccoon. When the world was made the Creator told all the creatures not to walk on the surface of the earth until the ground dried and got hard. But the raccoon didn't listen. He started digging in the soft land for crayfish. That was how the swamps were created. The Creator got mad at the raccoon and yelled at him that he wasn't supposed to do it. The raccoon started crying. His hands were black from digging in the mud and he wiped his eyes like this. That was how the raccoon got his black eyes."

WHERE LOVE BEGAN

"After the Creator made the animals He decided He would make man. Just like in the Bible. He took the clay and breathed into it and created man. The Bible says He breathed into his nostrils but we believe He breathed into his mouth. And the man started to breathe and became a living thing. Then the Creator gave him knowledge and wisdom, everything a man was supposed to have. But the man, he wasn't happy. He walked around the place with his head hung

down. One day the Creator said, 'I know why you're not happy—
you're lonesome, that's why.' So He put a deep sleep on the man,
and he took his bottom rib and made a woman out of it, and he put
the woman right beside the sleeping man. When the man woke up
he felt over like this with his hand and realized there was a person
lying beside him. He felt some more and he realized it was a woman!
So when he realized this he began to smile. And the woman—she
smiled at him, too. And that was where love began."

THE SORCERER'S CANE

On a second visit we bring an old wooden cane with a stylized reptile
carved into its handle. It was given to us by Santa Fe art dealer Fred
Kline, who suggested it was probably Seminole. Joe Jumper, the
middle-aged herbalist who has been interpreting Buffalo for us,
shakes his head at the cane. "Maybe Seminole, maybe not. I've
never seen one like it. Show it to Buffalo; he'll know." ✤ Sitting on
a bench outside his house, Buffalo takes the cane across his knees
and strokes it like a living thing. He stares at it hard. "Yes, it's
Seminole. Very old, from long before I was born. It was a chief's,
someone important. The carving looks maybe like an alligator—he
could have been alligator clan, but we don't have such a clan anymore. I think probably it's not alligator but a snake with legs. They
used to have those. A cane like this might be given to a visitor

through Seminole country. As long as he had it nobody would harm him. Today we don't have such canes anymore because we don't even own our own land. Sometimes I think we're only visitors here, too." ✤ Buffalo continues stroking the cane. "It still has power," he says. "The old man's power is still in it." ✤ The next day we return. Buffalo has kept the cane overnight and seems agitated. He tells us he had a dream last night. "A man came," he says, "a very old man, bent over, but very powerful. He wore deerskin trousers and a Seminole shirt, and he had a turban on his head. He was a medicine man, a sorcerer, a great chief of our people. It was the man who made this walking stick. His power is still in it, so take care. It can help you, but it can kill you, too." ✤ "Yes, a sorcerer. Maybe Coacoochee—Chief Wildcat himself. He was a real medicine man, much more powerful than Osceola. That was when our people fought the U.S. Army and we hid in the swamps. The army tricked us, arrested Osceola and Wildcat under a phony white flag of truce. They put them into the prison in St. Augustine. Osceola, he never got away; later they killed him. But Wildcat, he did magic. For four days he didn't eat anything. The soldiers laughed at him. They threw water at him. But on the fourth night he made the stone wall so soft that he reached his hands in like this and made a hole and let the people go through and he also squeezed the people small enough so they could go through that hole. Once they were out he told them to head south and he made it so the soldiers were like they were asleep and so the dogs couldn't bark and so the people made no tracks where their feet touched the ground. We had great leaders back then, leaders who could make a miracle, who knew the old Instructions. There won't be any more leaders like that. All be dead. Dead forever." ✤ With obvious reluctance he returns the cane. "Bring it back when you don't need it anymore," he says.

Years later, in 1989, we honor his request, returning the sorcerer's cane to the Seminole Tribe of Florida in honor of Buffalo Jim. James Billie, chairman of the Tribal Council, arranges a poignant ceremony in a large chickee at Big Cypress. Once again Buffalo lays the sorcerer's stick across his knees. His fingers lovingly stroke the time-burnished wood. With a fingernail he traces the carved reptile on the handle. He speaks again of Wildcat: "He could throw this stick on the ground and it would turn into a snake. And then he could turn it back into a stick. He had that power. Sometimes for good, sometimes for bad." ✠ After the ceremony, Chairman Billie asks Buffalo to "do some medicine" on the cane to ward off any evil influences that might still be lurking in it. Before we leave, Buffalo also prepares for us a jar of cold tea made of bitterroot and various leaves and herbs. He has us drink some of it and instructs us to splash the remainder over our heads and bodies for the next three days. "That old sorcerer might have worked some spell into the cane," he says. No doubt Wildcat had had little use for white men. Shortly before his death in 1857 he had said:

"I may be buried in the Earth or sunk in water,
but I shall go to the spirit of my sister and live with her.
Game is plentiful there.
And there the white man is never seen."

As we drive away from Big Cypress at nightfall down the dark expanse of Alligator Alley, a sense of well-being warms us—a vibrant inner awareness that we've had a personal part in bringing that cane back home, where it wanted to be, where it insisted on being. We feel at peace now with the sorcerer who made it—but are thankful nonetheless for Buffalo Jim's jar of protective medicine, fresh from the Everglades.

Tom Porter ✤ Mohawk

Tom Porter, Mohawk Chief of the Bear Clan at Akwasasne, New York, tells this true story about following the advice of the Old Ones.

A MODERN IROQUOIS LOVE STORY

My Grandmother was a seer. She came to me when I was 17 or 18, already at the age when my cousins were trying to take me to beer joints and stuff like that. My Grandmother was against that. She said, "If you care anything about me, you won't drink alcohol." Well, of course, I loved my Grandmother and there was no way I was going to bring shame on her. I told her I didn't do much drinking and didn't intend to start. She looked at me. She had a way of looking when she wanted to talk about important things. ✤ "Come here," she said. "There's something you've been thinking about pretty heavy." So I sat there at her table. She took a cup of some green tea. And she said: "We're going to find what's the problem, so it doesn't turn into an even bigger problem." She looked down into the cup. Her eyes opened wide, like she could see things in there, secret things, about the future. ✤ Now, my Grandmother, when she was inspired, always made a special sound. It sounded like *ohh-wahhhh-ahhh*. If the inspiration wasn't there, you wouldn't hear that sound. But if she was really inspired, you'd hear *ohh-wahhhh-ahhh*—like that. So this time I knew it was really important, because she held the cup of tea and stared down into it and said: *"Ohh-wahhhh-ahhh!"* ❖ She looked at me with that look. "So you're thinking about looking for a woman now, huh?" She looked down into the teacup again. *"Ohhhh!"* she said, "I can see a bunch of them in here! That's what you're thinking about now. Women!" Then she got a worried look on her face. She pointed into the teacup. "All kinds of women. But if you get the wrong one you're going to have big trouble. You've got to be careful." ❖ She squinted her eyes and pointed her finger into the cup. "Now," she said, "right here. Look at this one! A pretty girl. Nice complexion, just like a doll. She's got a nice shape. Nice curly hair. This girl will come over where you're standing and rub her chest up against your shoulder. And when she does—Oh! You won't know whether you're standing there frontwards or backwards, because a woman has power. Especially a young pretty woman. Well, you can say hello to her, but don't go much further than that . . . because, if you do, you're going to regret it. You'll cry every day for the rest of your life if you get serious and marry that girl. So you watch out for her!" ❖ Then my Grandmother pointed back in the teacup and said: "Oh, here's another one! She's a little taller, with straight hair. She'll rub her legs on your legs and you won't know nothing anymore but that lovely pair of legs. She looks like she's good, but she's only good for a little while. Then she's going to jump on your back, she's going to pull your hair and you're going to cry if you hook onto that one!" ❖ Again my Grandmother pointed in the cup. "Oh, and here's another one with a good shape, but a little bit heavy. And she really likes to laugh! She's going to hold your hand and swing you around. This one's going to take you to the bed right away. But, you watch out, she's a joker. She don't know how to be a mother or how to

cook or how to sew. She don't know how to do *nothing!* She's a dancer! Party and party and party, dance, have fun and laughter. That's all she's good for, so don't pay her any attention." ✤ Now my Grandmother looked down in the teacup again and swirled the dregs around real hard. And then she said: *"Ohh-wahhhh-ahhh!* Here's one, but, gee, she's only about that tall. This one's got black hair, jet black hair, and she sits on her hair when she sits down. Oh, she's got a nice shape, too, small but nice. She's standing all alone on the road and she's not going to jump on you. She can cook any-

thing, real Indian food, too. She can sew your clothes out of nothing, fix your stocking, and she likes to work all the time. She doesn't
like to talk much. She's the one for you." ✜ I asked my Grandmother, "Where does she live? Does she live over in Snye or St.
Regis or Cornwall Island? Or maybe Raquette Point?" My Grandmother said, "No, she's not from this place. She comes from quite a
distance from here." ✜ "Well," I said, "she must be an Onondaga
girl. Is she Onondaga?" "No," my Grandmother said, "it's way
toward where the sun goes down. You wait for that one! But, it's not
going to be next month, not next year, not two years. It's going to go
maybe up to ten years. But if you can wait for *that one,* you will never
cry all your married life. And you'll be happy, you'll never fight,
you'll have a perfect life together, *if you can just wait!* And when you
see this girl, she'll be walking on the road. And you will know her
just like that! You'll know *that's the one!"*

Well, just like she said, that's how it happened. I met the girl who
was laughing and laughing all the time, I met the one who put her
chest on my shoulder, and I met the one who rubbed my legs with
hers. I met them all. And I just narrowly escaped every one of them.
I was supposed to get married three different times, and each time,
as it came close, it never came about. Mostly because of my belief in
the Longhouse religion, the old religion. Two of the girls were
Christian. One was even Longhouse, but she wouldn't commit the
way I was committed. So I didn't marry any of them. I just waited.
✜ Years went by and I thought maybe I'd never marry. Finally one
day some guys and me were driving a mobile home down to Okla-
homa to have a meeting with the Choctaws. We were driving one of
the Choctaw men home from the meeting, and on that road we saw
these two girls walking. We drove by and they looked up, and right
away I said aloud: "There's my wife! Right there!" ✜ I should
have said it to myself, but I was just so surprised to see her! We

offered them a ride. They were two sisters—Choctaws. They were very shy and so was I. It turned out the girls' brother was going to ride down with us to Louisiana. The sisters began to cry when we got ready to go. I'd been making a beadwork necklace and I just gave it to her—the one I knew would be my wife. Her name was Alice. When I did that a great big tear came down her cheek. ✤ When we got to Louisiana, her brother, who couldn't write too well, said to me, "Tommy, can you write a letter for me to my mother to let her know I'm all right?" He told me what he wanted to say and I wrote it. Then I added a little piece of paper to his sister: "Hello, Alice. I hope you get this letter and everything's fine." That's all. ✤ Then a letter came back for the brother, and there was a note in there to me from Alice. It said, "Hello, Tom. I got your letter. Everything's fine. From Alice." That's all. So I wrote back again. This time I said, "Hello, Alice. I got your letter and I'm glad everything's fine. But this time I want to know if you're going to marry me. From Tom." ✤ About a week and half later I got another letter. It had a ten-dollar bill in it. The letter said, "Hello, Tom. That question you asked about getting married—I would like to. But I have to have a meeting with all my mother's sisters and brothers and they have to agree. Then I have to ask my father. If they all say yes, I will marry you. But if we get married, I want to get married Mohawk style, not Choctaw style, because the Choctaws drink too much at their wedding ceremonies, and you say the Mohawks don't do that. Meantime, here's ten dollars. If you see some pretty material for a Mohawk wedding dress, buy it. From Alice." ✤ Well, you know, we'd never even held hands! But I didn't have any doubt she was the one my Grandmother saw in the teacup. ✤ So I got the material, a beautiful navy-blue velveteen, and I made all of her wedding dress. We've still got it in the house. By the time we got back to Akwasasne I had finished that whole wedding dress. I told my mother, "Ma, I found the woman I want to marry." I was 26 years old already. I said, "It's up to you." ✤ In our way, if your mother says no, you can't marry. You have to have your mother's consent, and, in my case, my Grandmother's. My mother said, "Well, you're old enough, you should know your own self." ✤ Next I went to my

Grandmother. I said, "Grandmother, I've finally found that woman." She said, "Ahhhh, you mean that real Indian one? Well, you waited long enough. She must be the one." ✤ So, my aunt went to meet Alice's mother, get their family's agreement, and make the arrangements for the wedding. They decided on a date: November 7, 1970. Then one of my relatives died, so we had to cancel it. We set the date again, and then another relative died and we had to change it again. A third time we set the date and this time, the night before the wedding, one of my best friends—he'd been sewing my wedding shirt just that day—got killed in an auto accident. When I heard he got killed only a few hours before the wedding I started crying my head off. We had hundreds of pounds of food for the wedding, people had come in from all over, the Longhouse was packed with guests. ✤ My Grandmother said, "If you don't go through with it this time, then you must cancel the wedding forever. You two can never get married." So my aunts got together with the chiefs and made the decision. They talked to my dead friend's mother to see if it would be OK with her. She said yes and they told me, "Go ahead and get married." ✤ The wedding was scheduled for 11 a.m. Before it started my friend's mother stopped by and asked me if I could dress him in his burial clothes. I took my red wedding shirt—the one he'd sewn and admired so much—and we dressed him in it. I didn't get to the Longhouse for the wedding ceremony until 2 p.m. Everybody was crying. It was the saddest wedding there ever was.... ✤ After the wedding we went right with all the food to sit all night at my friend's wake. Next day he was buried in my red wedding shirt.

Been married nearly twenty years now. Got four kids. And we've never fought. We never argue. If I have to go to Onondaga and come home at two in the morning, my wife's there to open the door, smiling. She makes me a sandwich. And never do I hear, "Where the hell have you been?" She says, "You must be so tired now." It's always like that. She's the perfect wife. So I'm glad I listened to what my Grandmother told me. That's why I always say, "Follow the Old One's advice."

Thomas Banyacya ✛ Hopi

"**H**ere's where we go off the map," Tom Banyacya, Jr., announces as we head up a barely visible track through rough scrub brush into one of the most sacred landscapes in America—in Hopi belief, part of the very center of the Universe. This is Big Mountain on Black Mesa in northeast Arizona—where ancient sacred ceremonies are held that determine not only local rainfall but the very balance and harmony of Nature itself. We've come out to talk to Thomas Banyacya, Sr., the famed Interpreter of the Hopi prophecies, in New Oraibi on the Third Hopi Mesa, but first his son takes us on a "mandatory" tour of nearby Big Mountain and the so-called "Joint Use Area"—1.8 million acres of high-desert plateau where Navajo herders have lived on little-used Hopi land for generations. ✛ In 1972, the U.S. Congress passed Public Law 93-531, mandating that the Navajos in the Joint Use Area be relocated—ostensibly so Hopis could have the use of their own land. What seemed—to an unknowing American public—an eminently practical solution to the so-called "Hopi-Navajo Land Dispute" turned out to be the biggest forced relocation of human beings in the United States since the Japanese internment of World War II. It involved the erection of a 285-mile barbed wire fence and the compulsory removal of more than 10,000 Navajo Traditionalists to their "side" of the fence. When Navajo Elders raised their shotguns to stop the fencing crews in the early 1970s, thousands of Indian and white supporters—including most Traditionalist Hopis—joined a "Stop the Relocation" movement, which is still flourishing today. By 1990, four years after our first visit and the original 1986 "deadline" of PL 93-531, some 250 Navajo Traditionalist families still hold tena-

ciously to "this land where our umbilical cords are buried." ✤ "If you want to talk to my Dad," Tom Jr. explains, "you'll have to understand about Big Mountain. White Man just calls it "Joint Use Area." He doesn't realize this place is a Cathedral. It's our Jerusalem. It's also got some of the world's biggest deposits of coal, uranium, and oil shale—and that's why the big mining companies got Congress to pass a law relocating the Navajos who've lived out here for hundreds of years. They bill the whole thing as a 'Hopi-Navajo Land Dispute' and they get their puppet tribal councils to go along with it—but everyone knows why they want the Indians off the land...so they can get what's under it. Nobody's being fooled. But lots of people are being hurt." ✤ In a weathered one-room house far out in the scrub we visit three Navajo families living under a single sagging roof. An old grandmother, tears in her eyes, flails the air at the sight of us and starts half-screaming, half-crying in Navajo. "Your government, they stopped the water, they won't let us build a new room or even fix a broken windowpane! They took our sheep so we can't make wool for rugs and blankets anymore. They try to kill us off—but they never will!" ✤ We swing back through the scrub and up to Third Mesa for the first of several visits with Thomas Banyacya, Sr. It was in 1948 that the elders of Third Mesa appointed Banyacya and three other young men as their "ears and tongue" to tell the outside world of certain direful warnings contained in the Hopi prophecies: these warnings involved a "house of mica" (interpreted as the United Nations) and a "gourd-ful of ashes" (interpreted as the atomic bomb) and pointed to an inevitable universal conflagration—or "Purification"—unless mankind changed its destructive ways. Now in his early eighties, Thomas Banyacya—the only surviving Interpreter of the original four—remains one of the foremost spokesmen of the Traditionalist Indian movement.

THE FIRST PEOPLE

"We're the first people here. We're the aborigines of this continent. We live here with the permission of the Great Spirit. Now your Congress passes laws telling us where to live.

But the supreme law of the land is the Great Spirit's, not Man's Law.

Your Congress can't tell us where to live. Only the Great Spirit can do that."

THE GOURD OF ASHES

"There's no 'Hopi-Navajo Land Dispute.' There's only White Man's endless greed. We 'traditionals' don't recognize the Hopi and Navajo tribal councils that your government set up like puppets so they could sign away our land. It's all because the mining companies want the coal, and even more they want the uranium to create nuclear weapons. Our Prophecies speak of those weapons. They're called the Gourd of Ashes that the White Man will throw back and forth and there will be a fire in the sky that no one can put out. If you don't stop what you're doing, Nature will intervene. Other forces far beyond your control will come into play. The last stages are here now. All these earthquakes and volcanoes and fires and hurricanes—these are the final signs, the final warnings. These are the last stages. Our Prophecies tell us in the last stages the White Man will steal our lands. It's all happening now. We pray and meditate and ask the Great Spirit to keep the world together a while longer. But it's coming. The Purifiers are coming."

URANIUM & LIGHTNING

"We don't want these weapons made up of the uranium you take from our land. If you take the uranium the lightning won't come and bring the rains. The uranium attracts the lightning. Take it away and the lightning won't come. You have no right to take the lightning from us!"

GUARDIANS & CARETAKERS

"The Navajos help guard the land for the Hopi. We don't want them to leave. This is their sacred land, too. The White Man is the one who needs to leave before Nature intervenes. The Great Spirit made us caretakers of this land. We take care of it with our prayers and our ceremony. Now you poison it and rape it and destroy it with your strip mines and uranium tailings and power plants—all on sacred land! And you try to chase the last few Indians off so you can do your dirty work."

WHAT YOU CAN DO

"You ask me what you can do? I'll tell you. Repeal Public Law 93-531. We didn't pass it. You passed it. It's not our law, it's your law. It's your shame, not ours. You created it. Now you repeal it! There's still time. Tell your President, tell your Senators, tell your Congressmen—they must repeal this genocidal law!

> Let us live in peace and harmony to keep the land and all life in balance. Only prayer and meditation can do that."

THE CIRCLE & THE CROSS

"Our Prophecies tell of white people. They were once our brothers who went away to the East. They learned all about inventions there. They were supposed to come back here with the inventions and help us to a better life. They would complete our spiritual circle. But, instead of bringing the symbol of a circle, they brought the symbol of a cross. The circle brings people together, the cross sets them apart. The cross is a divider. And that's what they want to do to us Indian people. They want to hang us—on a cross of uranium!"

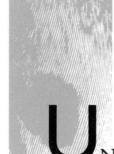

UNCLE FRANK DAVIS ✤ Pawnee

Too many chairs circle the rickety kitchen table—a table where everyone has a place, whether family, friends, or visiting strangers like ourselves. Over this oilcloth-covered formica tabletop, with its comforting coffee stains, tales have been told, gossip has been passed, grief has been expressed, and, above all, legends have been retold. Uncle Frank, as he's affectionately known—Fancy Warrior is his Indian name—takes his favorite seat and with a sweep of his hand gestures for us to sit down. He motions at the cold biscuits on the lazy Susan. "Plenty for everyone," he says. "Coffee's brewin.'"
✤ We've been told by several Pawnee that Uncle Frank is the pre-eminent local spiritual Elder—a leader of the peyote ceremony—but he denies any special knowledge. "We don't have real medicine men anymore," he says. "It's one thing to be a medicine man to whites, and another thing to Indians. I'm not even a chief and wouldn't want to be one." He's reluctant to speak about the peyote ceremony. "White people just don't understand it. There's nothing secret about peyote," he says. "It's just a sacred plant to help open the self up to receiving certain vibrations. It should never be abused. The plant would be offended. It could even kill you." He mentions he collects the peyote for his own ceremonies in Texas, and seems about to tell us more when he thinks better of it and waves a hand in the air, deflecting any further questions on the subject. ✤ His wife has recently died, and mementos to a long marriage fill every available

space on the walls. The windows are still draped in mourning. The house has remained almost untouched since her passing. Her absence is palpable. A telephone book sits on the chair that was hers—as if to discourage any thought of sitting there. A fine dust has settled over things, but it can't cover the emptiness she's left. Yet he smiles, genuinely happy to spin a yarn for a while instead of sitting by himself indulging sad memories. ✤ "So you've come about wisdom. Well, I'll tell you a story. Remember, it's just a story, though."

WISDOM'S PATH

"My mother was a good woman. I thought she was the wisest person in the whole world. So one day—when I was just a little feller, maybe six or seven—I asked her how I could become wise like her. She just laughed and laughed and said I was awfully young to be asking such questions. But, she said, since I asked, she would tell me." ✤ "'Life is like a path', she said, smiling down at me, 'and we all have to walk the path. If we lay down, we even lay down on that path. If we live through the night, we have to get up and start walking down that path again. As we walk down that path we'll find experiences like little scraps of paper in front of us along the way. We must pick up those pieces of scrap paper and put them in our pockets. Every single scrap of paper we come to should be put into that pocket. Then, one day, we will have enough scraps of papers to put together and see what they say. Maybe we'll have enough to make some sense. Read the information and take it to heart. Then put the pieces back in that pocket and go on, because there will be more pieces to pick up. Later we can pull them out and study them and maybe learn a little more. If we do this all through life, we'll know when to pull out those scraps to read more of the message. The more we read, the more we'll learn the meaning of life. We can become wise—or at least wiser than we were." ✚ Uncle Frank seems to be looking at his mother as he speaks, as if listening to her say those words spoken so long ago. "She said, 'But, if we never pick up those scraps of paper and never read them, we'll never become wiser. We'll keep on wondering about life and never learn the Creator's instructions. Remember one thing', she said with her finger pointed straight at me, 'even if we pick up all those scraps, we'll still be learning. Nobody ever learns all the answers.'" ✚ He leans forward in his chair. "I've always tried to pick up the scraps of paper, like my mother said." He smiles, almost chortling. "Missed a few, though. After that, some things just never made sense. Still trying to figure out what was on those missing scraps." ✚ Now he leans back. The smile fades. Tears brim in his eyes. "Last night I saw my wife," he murmurs. "She came in my sleep. I know it was her. She called my name. She was standing on the other side of a wide road. She said she wanted to be with me, but she couldn't get across the road. She said I'd have to be the one to cross the road if I wanted to be with her. She put her hand out. She's calling me." In the dim room his face is barely a silhouette against the draped window. A tear on his cheek catches a glint of light. "I miss her so. I think I'll be going over soon."

LEON SHENANDOAH ✤
Six Nations Iroquois Confederacy

He bears an ancient title, "Tadodaho"—presiding moderator or "Speaker of the House" of the fifty coequal "peace chiefs" comprising the Grand Council of the Six Nations Iroquois Confederacy in upper New York State. This still-living confederacy—composed originally of the Mohawk, the Seneca, the Onondaga, the Oneida, the Cayuga, and, later, the Tuscarora—was founded about 1000 A.D. by a prophet called the Peacemaker, who brought a "Great Law of Peace" to the then-warring Iroquois peoples. Only one obstacle stood in the way of a peaceful union: the original Tadodaho, a ferocious snake-haired Onondaga wizard who, after bitter resistance, was finally persuaded to join the Confederacy by the Peacemaker and his lieutenant Ayawentha, or Hiawatha (an Iroquois title erroneously applied to an Ojibway culture-hero in Longfellow's "Song of Hiawatha"). To appease the original Tadodaho and bring him into the fold, the Peacemaker made Onondaga the Confederacy's capital and named the fourteen chiefs of the Onondaga as "Keepers of the Central Fire"—a fire that burns to this day in the Onondaga Longhouse. ✤ Today, more than two hundred Tadodahos later, the venerable title and office have

devolved upon Leon Shenandoah, formerly subchief, or Faith-keeper, of the Eel clan of the Onondaga Nation. "I no longer serve a clan," he tells us. "The Tadodaho must give up his clan interests and serve all the people of the Confederacy." ✤ In 1971, shortly after becoming Tadodaho, he won national notice when he confronted New York State highway crews trying to add a lane to Interstate 81 where it slices through the Onondaga Nation's territory—some call it a "reservation"—just south of Syracuse.

Drawing a symbolic line with his ceremonial condolence cane across the road leading into Onondaga, Chief Shenandoah announced: "The United States stops here!" He then led a two-month sit-down on the construction site in a tense face-off against heavily armed state police. Negotiation finally won the day—the highway was widened, but only by a few feet—and a bloody showdown was narrowly averted. Ironically, the same state troopers involved at Onondaga were then dispatched to put down the infamous riot at Attica State Prison, where dozens of prisoners died in a hail of gunfire. ✤ "Those bullets were meant for us," Chief Shenandoah remembers. "The prisoners at Attica took the killing instead of us. That's the way it was with the buffalo, too. They took the killing instead of the Indian people. They died and we lived. If we'd taken *all* the killing, we wouldn't be here today." ✤ He sits at the dining room table in his cozy frame house, smoking a well-scuffed pipe. His smiling wife, Thelma, brings coffee to the two visitors. The sound of children's laughter—they have more than a dozen grandchildren, several of whom live here—echoes through the house. ✤ Alternately joking and falling into deep discussion, we broach the subject of confrontation: violent versus peaceful. "What is the greatest power?" we ask. Chief Shenandoah pauses, rapt in meditation, his eyes momentarily closed. Finally he speaks:

THE GREATEST STRENGTH

"I myself have no power. It's the people behind me who have the power. Real power comes only from the Creator. It's in His hands. But if you're asking about strength, not power, then I can say that the greatest strength is gentleness."

GIVING THANKS

"Our religion is all about thanking the Creator. That's what we do when we pray. We don't ask Him for things. We thank Him. We thank Him for the world and every animal and plant in it. We thank Him for everything that exists. We don't take it for granted that a tree's just there. We thank the Creator for that tree. If we don't thank Him, maybe the Creator'll take that tree away. That's what our ceremonies are about, that's why they're important—even for you, the White Man. We pray for the harmony of the whole world. We believe if we didn't do our ceremonies in the Longhouse the world would come to an end. It's our ceremonies that hold the world together. Some people may not believe that, they may laugh at it, but it's true. The Creator wants to be thanked. When we go in the Longhouse and thank Him for his Creation he kneels down and listens to us. He puts His ear to the Longhouse window. He hears his own children, so he holds off destroying the world for a while longer."

BEING WILD & BEING FREE

"If you white men had never come here, this country would still be like it was. It would be all pure here.

> You call it wild, but it wasn't really wild, it was free. Animals aren't wild, they're just free.

And that's the way we were. You called us wild, you called us savages. But we were just free! If we were savages, Columbus would never have gotten off this island alive."

WHAT'S COMING IS ALREADY HERE

"It's prophesied in our Instructions that the end of the world will be near when the trees start dying from the tops down. That's what the maples are doing today. Our Instructions say the time will come when there will be no corn, when nothing will grow in the garden, when the water will be filthy and unfit to drink. And then a great monster will rise up from the water and destroy mankind. One of the names of that monster is 'the sickness that eats you up inside'— like diabetes or cancer or AIDS. Maybe AIDS is the monster. It's coming. It's already here. Our Prophet Handsome Lake told of it in the 1700s. He saw Four Beings, like four angels, coming from the Four Directions. They told him what would happen, how there would be diseases we'd never heard of before. You will see many tears in this country. Then a great wind will come, a wind that will make a hurricane seem like a whisper. It will cleanse the earth and return it to its original state. That will be the punishment for what we've done to the Creation."

THE CREATOR'S GUESTS

"We are made from Mother Earth and we go back to Mother Earth. We can't 'own' Mother Earth. We're just visiting here. We're the Creator's guests. He's invited us to stay for a while, and now look what we've done to His Creation. We've poisoned it, we've made a wreck of it. He's bound to be mad—and He is."

WORKING FOR THE CREATION

"I'm working for the Creation. I refuse to take part in its destruction."

HOW WE LOST THE STARS

"White Man took the stars from us. Yeah, that's right, he stole the stars. Before White Man came we lived by the stars. The stars told us when to go hunting, when to go fishing. We had a name for every star. Then you came and gave us calendars and clocks and schedules and we forgot the stars. We don't read them anymore. Now we just follow the moon and the sun for our ceremonies and planting. We know only a little about where the stars are going to be or what they mean. That's all been lost. You guys took it from us. But where does it tell about that theft in your history books? You don't even know you stole it!"

THE ONLY PATH

"Everything is laid out for you. Your path is straight ahead of you. Sometimes it's invisible but it's there. You may not know where it's going, but still you have to follow that path. It's the path to the Creator. That's the only path there is."

ADDRESS TO THE GENERAL ASSEMBLY
OF THE UNITED NATIONS

Brothers, listen to the words of the Creator given to the first United Nations, the Haudenosaunee, over one thousand years ago. ✛ The Chiefs of the Haudenosaunee shall be mentors of the people for all time. The thickness of their skin shall be seven spans; which is to say that they shall be proof against anger, offensive action, and criticism. Their hearts shall be full of peace and good will and their minds filled with a yearning for the welfare of the people. With endless patience, they shall carry out their duty. Their firmness shall be tempered with a tenderness for their people. Neither anger nor fury shall find lodging in their minds, and all their words and actions shall be marked by calm deliberation. ✛ In every Nation there are wise and good men. These should be appointed Chiefs. They should be the advisers of their people and work for the good of all people, and all their power comes from the "Great Peace." A chief must never forget the Creator of mankind, never forget to ask Him for help. The Creator will guide our thoughts and strengthen us as we work to be faithful to our sacred trust and restore harmony among all peoples, all living creatures, and Mother Earth.... ✛ We were instructed to carry a love for one another and to show a great respect for all the beings of this earth.... ✛ In our ways, spiritual consciousness is the highest form of politics.... ✛ When people cease to respect and express gratitude for these many things, then all life will be destroyed, and human life on this planet will come to an end.

These are our times and our responsibilities. Every human being has a sacred duty to protect the welfare of our Mother Earth, from whom all life comes. In order to do this we must recognize the enemy—the one within us. We must begin with ourselves....

We must live in harmony with the Natural World and recognize that excessive exploitation can only lead to our own destruction. We cannot trade the welfare of our future generations for profit now. We must abide by the Natural Law or be victim of its ultimate reality. ✛ We must stand together, the four sacred colors of man, as the one family that we are in the interest of peace. ✤ We must abolish nuclear and conventional weapons of war. ✤ When warriors are leaders, you will have war. We must raise leaders of peace. ✤ We must unite the religions of the world as the spiritual force strong enough to prevail in peace.

It is no longer good enough to cry *peace*. We must act *peace*, live *peace*, and march in *peace* in alliance with the people of the world.

We are the spiritual energy that is thousands of times stronger than nuclear energy. Our energy is the combined will of *all* people with the spirit of the Natural World, to be of one body, one heart, and one mind for *peace*. ✤ We propose, as a resolution for peace, that October 24th be designated as a Day of Peace, and a worldwide cease-fire take place in honor of our children and the Seventh Generation to come.

Day nay toh,

TADODAHO CHIEF LEON SHENANDOAH HAUDENOSAUNEE
The Six Nations Iroquois Confederacy
October 25, 1985

DEWASENTA

Dewasenta, an Onondaga Clan Mother for over thirty years, is the sister of Tadodaho Leon Shenandoah. ✤ "When the chief of a clan falls—we say 'fall' instead of 'die'—that clan's Clan Mother and her family select a new chief. We don't vote—there has to be a consensus. Several names are usually brought up and we discuss each name. One name will rise and there will be a consensus." ✤ "The man who is to be chief must have certain qualifications. He must be a man who is honest. He must have 'Hoeyianah', or the 'good mind', as we say. He must have great concern and do the right thing by his people. He must not be a womanizer." ✤ "The Clan Mother can remove a chief. If he is guilty of 'forcing a woman'—we don't say 'rape'—or of stealing or of taking a life, the chief is deposed instantly, even without being forewarned." ✤ "If the chief shows signs of losing Hoeyianah, the good mind, the Clan Mother talks to him. She must give him three warnings. Then she, with the consent of the clan, can remove him. If she herself strays from the right path, the clan can remove her, also." ✤ "The role of Iroquois women remains today as it has always been. Some of our women have become Christian and see no value in the 'circle' of the Long-house. To be a Clan Mother, however, the woman must be within the Longhouse. Without her, the 'circle' would be broken."

IRVING POWLESS, SR. ✤ Onondaga

This is the famous "Thanksgiving Speech," spoken before important gatherings of the Six Nations Iroquois Confederacy. Each speaker gives it extempore. This version was delivered to an audience attending the 200th Anniversary of the Treaty of Fort Stanwyx in Rome, New York, in October 1984. Chief Powless, who has since passed on to the Creator, delivered it in the Onondaga language, and it is here rendered into English by his son, Chief Irving Powless, Jr.

LET US PUT OUR MINDS TOGETHER AS ONE

I want to greet you and to ask that we put our minds together as one and thank the Creator that we who have gathered here are all well. It is now my duty to give thanks.... ✤ The Creator has planned it this way—that, every time we meet, whether day or night, no matter how many or how few we are, we give thanks to Him for what He has given us. The Creator created the Earth, our Mother Earth, and gave her many duties, among them the duty to care for us, His people. He put things upon Mother Earth for the benefit of all. And as we travel around today we see that our Mother Earth is still doing her duty, and for that we are very grateful. So let us put our minds together as one and give thanks. And let it be that way.... ✤ The Creator planted grasses and weeds on Mother Earth. These grasses and weeds all have a name. Some of them are medicines. And as we pass through this year we see that the grasses and the weeds are still growing. So we are very grateful they are still here and doing their duties. Therefore let us put our minds together as one and give thanks to the grasses, the weeds, and the medicines. And let it be

that way.... ✤ The Creator also put trees and bushes upon Mother Earth for the benefit of all. Among the trees is the maple. From the maple tree we gather sap from which we make sugar and syrup. And as we pass through this year we see that the trees and the bushes are still there doing their duties. So let us put our minds together as one and be grateful that the trees and bushes are still there. And let it be that way.... ✤ The Creator put upon Mother Earth berries and plants for us to eat. All we have to do is pick them. The strawberries are the first to ripen each year. If we take the strawberry juice and drink it, it shall be a medicine for us. And as we pass through this year we see that the berries and plants are still doing their duties for the benefit of all. So let us all put our minds together as one and give thanks to the berries and plants for doing their duties. And let it be that way.... ✤ The Creator put animals on the earth. Animals give us food. They give us clothing. They even supply us with wampum for use in our ceremonies. The animals also have a leader. He is called the deer. And as we look about us and see that the animals are still here doing their duties, we are grateful and we give thanks. In our appreciation we put our minds together as one. And let it be that way.... ✤ The Creator also put upon Mother Earth the birds. He gave us small birds and large birds. The birds also have a duty. Their leader is the eagle. His duty is to fly high and watch over us. And the smaller birds have the duty to sing to us and also provide us with food. And as we look about us, let us give thanks to the birds, for they are still here doing their duties. They never tire and say, "I'm not going to do my duty anymore." And for that we are very grateful. So let us put our minds together as one and thank the birds. And let it be that way.... ✤ The Creator gave us life-giving foods. All we have to do is to plant seeds into Mother Earth and she will make them grow. This summer we've done this again, and the plants grew. And for this we are very grateful. So let us all put our minds together as one and give thanks to the foods that nourish us. And let our minds be that way.... ✤ The Creator gave us the wind. He makes sure it usually comes as a breeze, but every now and then He lets it come as a hurricane. That's to remind the people that they do not control the earth. And, as we see, the wind is still doing its duty. And for this we are grateful. So let us all put our minds together and give thanks to

the wind. And let our minds be that way.... ✤ The Creator, after He created all of these things, said, 'There needs to be more.' So he created the Thunderers, our Grandfathers. It shall be their duty to moisten and freshen the springs to replenish the fresh water that we drink. Last night I heard their thundering voices again. So we see that the Thunderers are still doing their duties. And for this we are very grateful. So let us all put our minds together as one and give thanks to the thundering voices. And let our minds be that way....
✤ The Creator gave us the sun, our elder brother. It's his duty to give us warmth and to nourish the life-giving foods that were planted on earth. And, as we see, the sun came up this morning and

shines on us, keeping us warm. He's doing his duty. And for this we are very grateful. So let us all put our minds together as one and thank the sun for still performing his duty. And let our minds be that way.... ✤ The Creator said we will have daylight and we will have darkness. The darkness will be for sleep and rest. But you will also have a night-sun which you will call the moon. The moon will be your Grandmother. And she will have special duties also. She will give moisture to dampen the land at night. She will also move the tides. Along with the moon there will be stars. The stars help give us directions when we travel and, along with Grandmother Moon, tell us when we should begin our ceremonies. The moon and the stars were put there for these purposes. And we see, last night, that the moon and the stars are still here doing their duties. And for this we are very grateful. So, in our appreciation, let us all put our minds together as one and give thanks to the stars and the moon. And let our minds be that way.... ✤ As the Creator looked over what he had created, He saw that many things could hurt our people, that many obstacles stood in our way. So He sent us four Protectors, four beings like angels who watch over us and help us when we need it. Often it happens that we find ourselves in dangerous situations. Then, somehow, we get out of it and it was only a close call. That's because the four Protectors are still watching over us and helping

us. And for that we are very grateful. So we put our minds together
as one and we thank the four Protectors for doing their duty. And
let our minds be that way.... ✚ Two centuries ago the Creator saw
that we were wandering from our ways because of the changes the
White Man had brought. So He sent us a Message through a chief
named Handsome Lake. His duty was to lead us back onto the Creator's path. Today his Message to us is still heard in our Longhouse.
We remember every word. And we are very grateful for that. So let
us all put our minds together as one and thank Handsome Lake for
doing his duty. And let our minds be that way.... ✚ When the
Creator created us, He used a part of His heart in each one of us.
And He wants his heart to return to Him. So each day and each
night He sends down His love to us. And He asks that we carry out
the duties that we were directed to perform. And for this we are very
grateful. So let us put our minds together as one and try to be the
people that He wants us to be. And let it be that way....

LOUIS FARMER ✦ Onondaga

It took us quite a while to get to know Onondaga Chief Louis Farmer. We saw him frequently around the Longhouse and at social gatherings for several years. He would sit somewhere by himself, seemingly scowling whenever we glanced his way. But we noticed people were always coming over to him—chatting, laughing, whispering. He was obviously well-beloved. His scowls were purely for outsiders, as if to say, "Don't bother me. I've got enough to do taking care of my own people." Then, one day in May 1986, our friend Maisie Shenandoah, a Clan Mother at the 32-acre Oneida Territory, called us and asked if we could drive one of the chiefs out from Onondaga, 35 miles away, so he could bless the site of their new Longhouse as well as the planting of the "Three Sisters"—corn, beans, and squash—which are the traditional staples of Iroquois diet. The chief was Louis Farmer. It was the opportunity we had been looking for. ✦ We picked Louis up at his centuries-old log cabin and drove him out to Oneida Territory, where we spent a wonderful day with him and Maisie. Of the many things this Wisdomkeeper told us, we especially remember these:

ON BEING A CHIEF

"We chiefs are the keepers of the Central Fire. But it's not just a fire
of logs and flames. It's the fire in here (he pointed to his own heart
with a gnarly finger) and also the fire in here (he tapped his fore-
head).

A good heart and a good mind—those are what you need to be
a chief."

ON TELEPHONES & TOBACCO

"Who needs a telephone? This (he took a pinch of tobacco from a pouch) is my communication. Better than any telephone. Telephones carry your voice around the earth, not up to the Creator. You don't need a telephone to talk to the Creator. When we want to talk to Him we burn tobacco and it takes our prayers all the way up to the Sky World. What telephone can do that?"

ON INDIAN RELIGION VS. WHITE MAN'S RELIGION

"White Man celebrates something that happened 2,000 years ago. To him, nothing's happened since then. It's all over. All he can do is remember. Indians celebrate what's happening now. When the sacred strawberries come up in early spring, that's what we celebrate. They're not just strawberries to us. They're the Creator's gift to his children. They're good to eat, good to drink. But more than that, they have the Creator's power in them. They make us healthy and strong. And we know, when we pass on, that our path to the Sky World will be lined with strawberries. So strawberries are more than just plants to us. That's why every year we have our Strawberry Thanksgiving—it's something that's happening now—to us—not something that happened long ago to somebody else." ✚

"In late spring we plant the corn and beans and squash. They're not just plants—we call them the Three Sisters. We plant them together, three kinds of seeds in one hole. They want to be together with each other, just as we Indians want to be together with each other. So long as the Three Sisters are with us we know we will never starve. The Creator sends them to us each year. We celebrate them now. We thank Him for the gift He gives us today and every day. He didn't stop giving us His gifts 2,000 years ago."

RUNNING IN THE WOODS

"When someone, an Indian, gets caught between the Longhouse religion and Christianity—when they don't follow either one or the other—we say, 'They're running in the woods.' They don't have a home either here or there, either in Indian's world or White Man's world. They don't pay attention to the Creator, so they've got to keep running—even though they've got nowhere to go. That's a terrible thing."

ON MEDICINE MEN

"You want to know who's a real medicine man? He's the one who doesn't say 'I'm a medicine man.' He doesn't ask you to come to him. You've got to go and ask him. And you'll find he's always there among his own people.

He doesn't go off to the city and open an office. Once a medicine man leaves his own territory, he loses most of his power. All the sacred plants he knows are where he comes from. He doesn't know the plants of other places. The Creator gave him his gift so he could serve his own people, not somebody else. The people he's supposed to help are people where he's from. So he stays home and helps them. That's who a real medicine man is."

EPILOGUE ✤ Unto the Seventh Generation

Our journey into Native America began with a heavy burden of misconceptions and stereotypes—gleaned from history books, movie Westerns, and popular myths ingrained in the psyche from an earlier "Manifest Destiny" mentality. What we thought we were going out to "discover" turned out to be far different from what we found. We uncovered no "secrets," no soul-bewitching gurus, no miraculous healers, no hitherto unknown sacred ceremonies. Life itself, we learned, is a sacred ceremony. From the Wisdomkeepers we learned a different way of thinking, which profoundly affected our views about the Earth, about sovereignty, about family and community, and about the future. ✤ The future, we learned, was not some abstract, untouchable "Beyond" far out there somewhere, beyond our ken. Rather, the Wisdomkeepers taught us, the future is with us here today, in the Now and Here. It's coming up, in fact, right behind us. Over and over we were told: Turn around and look, there they are, the Seventh Generation—they're coming up right behind you. "Look over your shoulder," Tadodaho Leon Shenandoah told us.

"Look behind you. See your sons and your daughters. They are your future. Look farther, and see your sons' and your daughters' children and their childrens' children even unto the Seventh Generation. That's the way we were taught. Think about it: you yourself are a Seventh Generation!"

This immediate and compassionate approach to the future was a revelation to us, moving us from a mental position to which we can never return. We came to realize that we ourselves, in all of our decisions—individually and collectively—are responsible for, and to,

the generations "whose faces are coming from beneath the ground." They will soon be walking the same earthly path we walk today, and we must ensure that there is a path to walk. We hope that we'll leave a better path than the one left to us.

Contrary to the popular notion that the traditional circle is dying away, we saw emerging Wisdomkeepers in action. Spiritual Elder Leila Fisher of the Hoh died in 1986. During a recent kitchen-table conversation that lasted into the wee hours of the morning and took us through many cups of strong black coffee, Leila's daughter, Mary Leitka, spoke of her mother. ✤ "Mom always told me I would have to prepare myself, and she said she would help me. But when she died it seemed she'd never really gotten around to properly instructing me. She knew so much and I know so little. Yet I'm hearing her words over and over in my thoughts. "She said there are two ways to go: the way of the Black Face—a society within our culture—or another way that is more personal—like going and bathing in the river every morning, sitting and meditating at a special place. 'Merge into Nature,' she would say. 'Merge into the spirit of the river, of the eagle, of the salmon.' This way would lead me to my power, or 'Help', as we say." ✤ During the funeral and the burning of all of Leila Fisher's personal belongings (as is the custom of the Hoh so that there is nothing to hold the one who has passed away to this world), Mary was told by the few remaining family Elders that she was the one to sing her mother's song during the proceedings. Mary adds, "It was my grandfather's song, and he passed it to my mother. Pansy Hudson, an Elder, told me that I was to have the family song after Mom died." ✤ "Now everyone looks to me. I don't know why, and it's very hard on me. They don't know where to turn, so they come to me like I'm supposed to know what to do. I have seven children and all their friends come here. Everyone is calling me 'Auntie.' They're welcome—but it's so hard. I'm at a crossroads. I see what's happening, and I wish so much that Mom was here." ✤ Before passing, Leila told Mary, "Take care of my grandchildren, all of them." Today Mary is teaching the youth the ancient songs and dances, passing along the stories of the Hoh which she learned in her own childhood. She says, "Maybe it boils down to my accepting the idea that Mom really gave me something and did prepare me all along through my life without my knowing what she was doing."

One bright June day an entire Oneida clan climbed a hill near their community in upstate New York. There was the Elder leading the way, and behind him were his children, nieces and nephews, followed by grandchildren and grandnieces and grandnephews—generation by generation, down to the infants in traditional baby boards. Atop the hill they posed for a photograph by "making circle," a traditional activity in which family members honor the Elder by recognizing his or her central position in the family. Throughout our travels in search of the Wisdomkeepers we kept seeing aspects of that same sacred circle or sacred hoop—one of the fundamental symbols of Native American culture. ✤ There's the cycle or circle of the seasons, the circle of the ceremonies, the family circle, the circle of the community, the circle of Elders, the cycle of the generations, and the circle of all life, of which mankind is only one aspect—all things *one*. ✤ Yes, we are changed.

POSTSCRIPT

Every part of this country is sacred to my people.... The very dust responds more lovingly to our footsteps than to yours, because it is the ashes of our ancestors.... ✚ There was a time when our people covered the land as the waves of a wind-ruffled sea cover its shell-paved floor. But that time long since passed away with the greatness of tribes that are now but a mournful memory.... ✚ And when the last Red Man shall have perished from this Earth and the memory of my tribe shall have become a myth among the White Men, these shores will swarm with the invisible dead of my tribe.... ✚ And when your children's children think themselves alone in the field, the store, the shop, upon the highway or in the silence of the pathless woods, they will not be alone.... ✚ At night when the streets of your cities and villages are silent and you think them deserted, they will throng with the returning hosts that once filled and still love this beautiful land.... ✚ The White Man will never be alone.... ✚ Let him be just and deal kindly with my people, for the dead are not powerless.... ✚ Dead, did I say? There is no death, only a change of worlds!

CHIEF SEATTLE, 1855

PHOTOGRAPHER'S NOTES

CHARLIE KNIGHT

15 · According to Ute belief, surrounding mesas and buttes contain the spirit of a giant ancestral warrior who will rise to defend his people in a time of crisis. At his remote little camp amid the panoramic landscape, Ute medicine man Charlie Knight trains horses, raises sheep, and catches wild bulls for sale at the livestock auction in nearby Cortez, Colorado.

FRANK FOOLS CROW

21 · Lakota ceremonial priest Frank Fools Crow officiates at the Tenth Anniversary of the occupation of Wounded Knee by American Indian Movement activists in 1973. Marching from the sacred Four Directions, celebrants converge on the site of the ceremony, held in February 1983 on the Pine Ridge Reservation in South Dakota.

MATHEW KING

35 · Bear Butte, holy mountain of the Lakota, rises amid the Black Hills, which were promised to the Lakota "forever" until gold was discovered there in 1868.

36 · Lakota spiritual Elder Mathew King poses for this double-portrait with a sepia-tone photograph of his grandfather.

EDDIE BENTON-BANAI

52 · At a 1984 spiritual encampment on the shores of Lake Superior, Ojibway educator Eddie Benton-Banai—fourth-level Midewiwin priest and founder of the Red School House in St. Paul—teaches young followers how to build a sacred lodge of bent saplings in the manner of their ancestors.

55 · The day begins with a prayer—beaten out on the sacred drum—at the Red School House. "Teach the children," Eddie counsels his people, "...They're the Grandfathers and Grandmothers of tomorrow."

97 · A Navajo child on the Hopi-
Navajo Joint Use Area clings to
a controversial barbed wire
fence—erected by the government
to separate Navajo and Hopi
Traditionalists who have lived
here together for more than
a century.

LEON SHENANDOAH

103 · Hands of Tadodaho Leon
Shenandoah—presiding chief of
the Six Nations Iroquois—hold
the eagle-headed ceremonial staff
of office of the Confederacy.
Pegs and pictographs recall the
fifty peace chiefs of the original
centuries-old Confederacy.

104 · At an annual ceremony in
Canandaigua, New York, Chief
Shenandoah holds aloft a wampum belt commemorating the
1794 Canandaigua Treaty between the Iroquois Confederacy
and the fledgling United States.

105 · Six Nations chiefs, seated in the
longhouse at Onondaga, receive
sacred wampum belts returned to
the Confederacy by New York
State in a moving ceremony
in 1989.

108 · Onondaga clan mother Dewasenta and Chief Shenandoah—
brother and sister—enjoy the
company of the coming
generation.

IRVING POWLESS

114 · New York State Museum Direc-
tor Martin Sullivan transfers
ownership of sacred wampum
back to Onondaga Chief Irving
Powless, Jr., who accepts on
behalf of the Six Nations
Iroquois Confederacy.

LOUIS FARMER

117 · Awaiting his ride to the new
Longhouse groundbreaking
ceremonies at Oneida Territory—
where he will officiate—Louis
Farmer stands in front of his one-
room house at Onondaga.

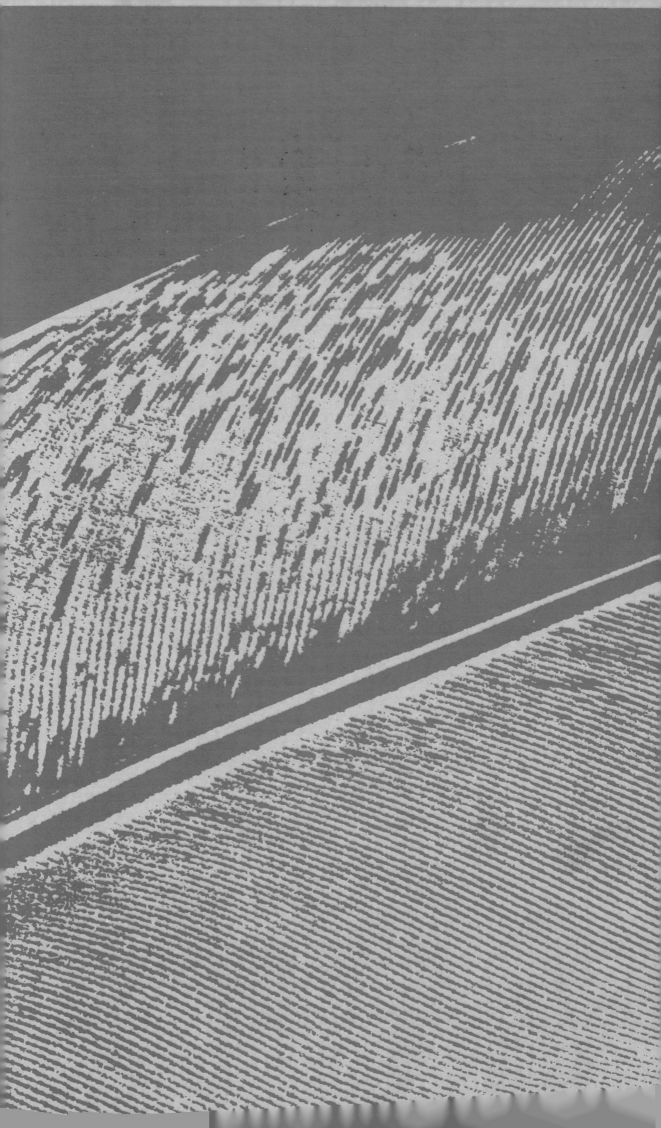